45 Cake Recipes for Home

By: Kelly Johnson

Table of Contents

Recipes

- Classic Chocolate Cake:
    - Moist chocolate layers with chocolate ganache.
- Vanilla Bean Cake:
    - Light and fluffy vanilla cake with real vanilla beans.
- Red Velvet Cake:
    - Signature red velvet layers with cream cheese frosting.
- Lemon Blueberry Cake:
    - Zesty lemon cake filled with blueberries.
- Carrot Cake:
    - Spiced carrot cake topped with cream cheese icing.
- Coconut Pineapple Cake:
    - Coconut-flavored cake with pineapple filling.
- Strawberry Shortcake:
    - Layers of vanilla cake, fresh strawberries, and whipped cream.
- Marble Cake:
    - Swirled chocolate and vanilla cake.
- Pumpkin Spice Cake:
    - Perfect for fall, with pumpkin and warm spices.
- Hummingbird Cake:
    - Banana and pineapple cake with cream cheese frosting.
- Raspberry Almond Cake:
    - Almond-flavored cake with raspberry filling.
- Oreo Cheesecake Cake:
    - Layers of Oreo cheesecake and chocolate cake.
- Mint Chocolate Chip Cake:
    - Mint-flavored cake with chocolate chips.
- Peanut Butter Cup Cake:
    - Chocolate cake with peanut butter cup filling.
- Tiramisu Cake:
    - Coffee-flavored cake with mascarpone frosting.
- Caramel Apple Cake:
    - Apple-spiced cake with caramel drizzle.
- Cherry Chocolate Cake:
    - Chocolate cake with cherry filling.

- Almond Joy Cake:
    - Coconut and almond cake with chocolate ganache.
- Lavender Lemon Cake:
    - Floral lavender cake with lemon frosting.
- Maple Pecan Cake:
    - Pecan-studded cake with maple frosting.
- Coffee and Walnut Cake:
    - Coffee-infused cake with walnut pieces.
- Mango Coconut Cake:
    - Tropical flavors with mango and coconut.
- Hazelnut Chocolate Cake:
    - Nutella-inspired cake with hazelnuts.
- Cinnamon Roll Cake:
    - Swirled cinnamon and sugar layers.
- Guinness Chocolate Cake:
    - Moist chocolate cake with a hint of Guinness.
- Chai Spiced Cake:
    - Warm spices like cinnamon, cardamom, and ginger.
- Cranberry Orange Cake:
    - Tangy orange cake with cranberry filling.
- Rum Raisin Cake:
    - Rummy cake with plump raisins.
- Black Forest Cake:
    - Chocolate cake with cherries and whipped cream.
- Passion Fruit Cake:
    - Tropical and tangy passion fruit flavor.
- Pistachio Rose Cake:
    - Pistachio-flavored cake with a hint of rose.
- S'mores Cake:
    - Layers of graham cracker, chocolate, and marshmallow.
- Buttermilk Honey Cake:
    - Moist and sweet with buttermilk and honey.
- Matcha Green Tea Cake:
    - Earthy matcha-flavored cake.
- Pineapple Upside-Down Cake:
    - Classic upside-down cake with pineapple.
- Lemon Poppy Seed Cake:
    - Light lemony cake with poppy seeds.
- Cappuccino Cake:
    - Coffee-flavored layers with cappuccino frosting.

- Chocolate Raspberry Cake:
    - Rich chocolate cake with raspberry filling.
- Key Lime Pie Cake:
    - Tangy key lime flavor in cake form.
- Mocha Hazelnut Cake:
    - Coffee and hazelnut-infused cake.
- Banana Nutella Cake:
    - Banana cake with Nutella swirls.
- Mint Oreo Cake:
    - Mint-flavored cake with Oreo pieces.
- Caramel Macchiato Cake:
    - Coffee and caramel layers.
- Gingerbread Cake:
    - Warm spices of gingerbread in cake form.
- Chocolate Peanut Butter Cake:
    - Indulgent layers of chocolate and peanut butter.

Classic Chocolate Cake

Ingredients:

For the Cake:

- 2 cups all-purpose flour
- 1¾ cups granulated sugar
- ¾ cup unsweetened cocoa powder
- 1½ teaspoons baking powder
- 1½ teaspoons baking soda
- 1 teaspoon salt
- 2 large eggs, at room temperature
- 1 cup whole milk
- ½ cup vegetable oil
- 2 teaspoons pure vanilla extract
- 1 cup boiling water

For the Chocolate Ganache:

- 1 cup semisweet or bittersweet chocolate chips
- ½ cup heavy cream
- 2 tablespoons unsalted butter

Instructions:

For the Cake:

> Preheat your oven to 350°F (175°C). Grease and flour two 9-inch round cake pans.
> In a large mixing bowl, sift together the flour, sugar, cocoa powder, baking powder, baking soda, and salt.
> Add the eggs, milk, oil, and vanilla extract to the dry ingredients. Beat on medium speed for 2 minutes until well combined.
> Stir in the boiling water until the batter is smooth. The batter will be thin, but that's okay.
> Pour the batter evenly into the prepared pans. Bake in the preheated oven for 30 to 35 minutes or until a toothpick inserted into the center comes out clean.
> Allow the cakes to cool in the pans for 10 minutes, then transfer them to a wire rack to cool completely.

For the Chocolate Ganache:

In a small saucepan, heat the heavy cream over medium heat until it just begins to simmer.
Place the chocolate chips in a heatproof bowl. Pour the hot cream over the chocolate and let it sit for a minute.
Add the butter to the bowl and stir the mixture until smooth and glossy.
Allow the ganache to cool slightly before spreading it over the cooled chocolate cake.
Optionally, you can let the ganache set for a more firm texture or serve it immediately for a glossy finish.

Enjoy your classic chocolate cake! You can also add decorations like chocolate shavings or sprinkles for an extra touch.

Vanilla Bean Cake

Ingredients:

For the Cake:

- 2 ½ cups all-purpose flour
- 2 ½ teaspoons baking powder
- ½ teaspoon salt
- 1 cup unsalted butter, softened
- 2 cups granulated sugar
- 4 large eggs
- 1 tablespoon pure vanilla extract
- Seeds scraped from 1 vanilla bean
- 1 ½ cups whole milk

For Vanilla Bean Buttercream:

- 1 cup unsalted butter, softened
- 4 cups confectioners' sugar, sifted
- 2 teaspoons pure vanilla extract
- Seeds scraped from 1 vanilla bean
- 3-4 tablespoons whole milk

Instructions:

For the Cake:

Preheat your oven to 350°F (175°C). Grease and flour three 8-inch round cake pans.
In a medium bowl, whisk together the flour, baking powder, and salt. Set aside.
In a large mixing bowl, cream together the softened butter and granulated sugar until light and fluffy.
Add the eggs one at a time, beating well after each addition. Mix in the vanilla extract and the scraped seeds from the vanilla bean.
Gradually add the dry ingredients to the wet ingredients, alternating with the milk. Begin and end with the dry ingredients, mixing just until combined.
Divide the batter evenly among the prepared cake pans and smooth the tops with a spatula.
Bake in the preheated oven for 25-30 minutes or until a toothpick inserted into the center comes out clean.

Allow the cakes to cool in the pans for 10 minutes before transferring them to a wire rack to cool completely.

For Vanilla Bean Buttercream:

In a large mixing bowl, beat the softened butter until creamy and smooth.
Add the sifted confectioners' sugar, vanilla extract, and the scraped seeds from the vanilla bean. Mix on low speed until combined.
Gradually add the milk, one tablespoon at a time, until you reach your desired consistency.
Beat the buttercream on medium-high speed for 3-5 minutes until light and fluffy.

Assembling the Cake:

Place one cake layer on a serving plate. Spread a layer of vanilla bean buttercream on top.
Add the second cake layer and repeat the process. Place the third layer on top.
Use the remaining buttercream to frost the top and sides of the cake.
Optional: Garnish with additional vanilla bean seeds or decorations of your choice.

Slice and enjoy your delightful Vanilla Bean Cake!

Red Velvet Cake

Ingredients:

For the Cake:

- 2 ½ cups all-purpose flour
- 1 ½ cups granulated sugar
- 1 teaspoon baking powder
- 1 teaspoon baking soda
- 1 teaspoon cocoa powder
- 1 ½ cups vegetable oil
- 1 cup buttermilk, at room temperature
- 2 large eggs, at room temperature
- 2 tablespoons red food coloring
- 1 teaspoon pure vanilla extract
- 1 teaspoon white vinegar or apple cider vinegar

For Cream Cheese Frosting:

- 16 ounces (450g) cream cheese, softened
- ½ cup (1 stick) unsalted butter, softened
- 4 cups confectioners' sugar, sifted
- 1 teaspoon pure vanilla extract

Instructions:

For the Cake:

Preheat your oven to 350°F (175°C). Grease and flour two 9-inch round cake pans.
In a large mixing bowl, sift together the flour, sugar, baking powder, baking soda, and cocoa powder.
In a separate bowl, whisk together the oil, buttermilk, eggs, red food coloring, vanilla extract, and vinegar.
Add the wet ingredients to the dry ingredients and mix until well combined. Be careful not to overmix.
Divide the batter evenly between the prepared cake pans and smooth the tops with a spatula.
Bake in the preheated oven for 25-30 minutes or until a toothpick inserted into the center comes out clean.

Allow the cakes to cool in the pans for 10 minutes before transferring them to a wire rack to cool completely.

For Cream Cheese Frosting:

In a large mixing bowl, beat the softened cream cheese and butter until creamy and smooth.
Add the sifted confectioners' sugar and vanilla extract. Beat on low speed until combined, then increase the speed to medium-high and beat until light and fluffy.

Assembling the Cake:

Place one cake layer on a serving plate. Spread a layer of cream cheese frosting on top.
Add the second cake layer and repeat the process.
Use the remaining cream cheese frosting to frost the top and sides of the cake.
Optional: Decorate with red velvet cake crumbs, if desired.

Slice and enjoy your classic Red Velvet Cake!

Lemon Blueberry Cake

Ingredients:

For the Cake:

- 2 ½ cups all-purpose flour
- 2 teaspoons baking powder
- ½ teaspoon baking soda
- ½ teaspoon salt
- 1 cup unsalted butter, softened
- 1 ¾ cups granulated sugar
- 4 large eggs
- 1 tablespoon lemon zest (from about 2 lemons)
- 2 tablespoons fresh lemon juice
- 1 teaspoon pure vanilla extract
- 1 cup buttermilk
- 2 cups fresh blueberries (tossed in 1 tablespoon of flour to prevent sinking)

For Lemon Cream Cheese Frosting:

- 8 ounces (225g) cream cheese, softened
- ½ cup (1 stick) unsalted butter, softened
- 4 cups confectioners' sugar, sifted
- 1 tablespoon fresh lemon juice
- 1 teaspoon lemon zest

Instructions:

For the Cake:

> Preheat your oven to 350°F (175°C). Grease and flour three 8-inch round cake pans.
> In a medium bowl, whisk together the flour, baking powder, baking soda, and salt. Set aside.
> In a large mixing bowl, cream together the softened butter and granulated sugar until light and fluffy.
> Add the eggs one at a time, beating well after each addition. Mix in the lemon zest, lemon juice, and vanilla extract.
> Add the dry ingredients to the wet ingredients in three additions, alternating with the buttermilk. Begin and end with the dry ingredients, mixing just until combined.
> Gently fold in the blueberries coated in flour to prevent them from sinking.

Divide the batter evenly among the prepared cake pans and smooth the tops with a spatula.

Bake in the preheated oven for 25-30 minutes or until a toothpick inserted into the center comes out clean.

Allow the cakes to cool in the pans for 10 minutes before transferring them to a wire rack to cool completely.

For Lemon Cream Cheese Frosting:

In a large mixing bowl, beat the softened cream cheese and butter until creamy and smooth.

Add the sifted confectioners' sugar, lemon juice, and lemon zest. Beat on low speed until combined, then increase the speed to medium-high and beat until light and fluffy.

Assembling the Cake:

Place one cake layer on a serving plate. Spread a layer of lemon cream cheese frosting on top.

Add the second cake layer and repeat the process. Place the third layer on top.

Use the remaining lemon cream cheese frosting to frost the top and sides of the cake.

Optional: Garnish with additional blueberries and lemon zest for decoration.

Slice and enjoy your delightful Lemon Blueberry Cake!

Carrot Cake

Ingredients:

For the Cake:

- 2 cups all-purpose flour
- 2 cups granulated sugar
- 1 teaspoon baking powder
- ½ teaspoon baking soda
- ½ teaspoon salt
- 1 teaspoon ground cinnamon
- ½ teaspoon ground nutmeg
- ½ cup vegetable oil
- ½ cup unsweetened applesauce
- 4 large eggs
- 1 teaspoon vanilla extract
- 2 cups finely grated carrots (about 4 medium carrots)
- 1 cup crushed pineapple, drained
- ½ cup shredded coconut
- ½ cup chopped walnuts or pecans (optional)

For Cream Cheese Frosting:

- 8 ounces (225g) cream cheese, softened
- ½ cup (1 stick) unsalted butter, softened
- 4 cups confectioners' sugar, sifted
- 1 teaspoon vanilla extract

Instructions:

For the Cake:

Preheat your oven to 350°F (175°C). Grease and flour two 9-inch round cake pans.
In a medium bowl, whisk together the flour, sugar, baking powder, baking soda, salt, cinnamon, and nutmeg.
In a large mixing bowl, whisk together the oil, applesauce, eggs, and vanilla extract until well combined.
Gradually add the dry ingredients to the wet ingredients, mixing until just combined.
Fold in the grated carrots, crushed pineapple, shredded coconut, and chopped nuts (if using).

Divide the batter evenly between the prepared cake pans and smooth the tops with a spatula.

Bake in the preheated oven for 25-30 minutes or until a toothpick inserted into the center comes out clean.

Allow the cakes to cool in the pans for 10 minutes before transferring them to a wire rack to cool completely.

For Cream Cheese Frosting:

In a large mixing bowl, beat the softened cream cheese and butter until creamy and smooth.

Add the sifted confectioners' sugar and vanilla extract. Beat on low speed until combined, then increase the speed to medium-high and beat until light and fluffy.

Assembling the Cake:

Place one cake layer on a serving plate. Spread a layer of cream cheese frosting on top.

Add the second cake layer and repeat the process.

Use the remaining cream cheese frosting to frost the top and sides of the cake.

Optional: Garnish with additional chopped nuts or shredded carrots for decoration.

Slice and enjoy your delicious and moist Carrot Cake!

Coconut Pineapple Cake

Ingredients:

For the Cake:

- 2 ½ cups all-purpose flour
- 2 ½ teaspoons baking powder
- ½ teaspoon baking soda
- ½ teaspoon salt
- 1 cup unsalted butter, softened
- 2 cups granulated sugar
- 4 large eggs
- 1 teaspoon coconut extract
- 1 cup coconut milk
- 1 cup crushed pineapple, drained
- ½ cup shredded coconut

For Coconut Cream Cheese Frosting:

- 8 ounces (225g) cream cheese, softened
- ½ cup (1 stick) unsalted butter, softened
- 4 cups confectioners' sugar, sifted
- 1 teaspoon coconut extract
- ½ cup shredded coconut (for decoration)

Instructions:

For the Cake:

> Preheat your oven to 350°F (175°C). Grease and flour three 8-inch round cake pans.
> In a medium bowl, whisk together the flour, baking powder, baking soda, and salt. Set aside.
> In a large mixing bowl, cream together the softened butter and granulated sugar until light and fluffy.
> Add the eggs one at a time, beating well after each addition. Mix in the coconut extract.
> Add the dry ingredients to the wet ingredients in three additions, alternating with the coconut milk. Begin and end with the dry ingredients, mixing just until combined.
> Fold in the crushed pineapple and shredded coconut.
> Divide the batter evenly among the prepared cake pans and smooth the tops with a spatula.

Bake in the preheated oven for 25-30 minutes or until a toothpick inserted into the center comes out clean.

Allow the cakes to cool in the pans for 10 minutes before transferring them to a wire rack to cool completely.

For Coconut Cream Cheese Frosting:

In a large mixing bowl, beat the softened cream cheese and butter until creamy and smooth.

Add the sifted confectioners' sugar and coconut extract. Beat on low speed until combined, then increase the speed to medium-high and beat until light and fluffy.

Assembling the Cake:

Place one cake layer on a serving plate. Spread a layer of coconut cream cheese frosting on top.

Add the second cake layer and repeat the process. Place the third layer on top.

Use the remaining coconut cream cheese frosting to frost the top and sides of the cake.

Optional: Sprinkle shredded coconut on top for decoration.

Slice and enjoy your delicious Coconut Pineapple Cake with tropical flavors!

Strawberry Shortcake

Ingredients:

For the Shortcakes:

- 2 cups all-purpose flour
- 1/4 cup granulated sugar
- 1 tablespoon baking powder
- 1/2 teaspoon salt
- 1/2 cup (1 stick) unsalted butter, cold and cut into small pieces
- 2/3 cup whole milk
- 1 teaspoon vanilla extract

For the Strawberries:

- 4 cups fresh strawberries, hulled and sliced
- 1/4 cup granulated sugar (adjust to taste)
- 1 teaspoon balsamic vinegar (optional, for enhanced flavor)

For the Whipped Cream:

- 1 cup heavy cream
- 2 tablespoons powdered sugar
- 1 teaspoon vanilla extract

Instructions:

For the Shortcakes:

> Preheat your oven to 425°F (220°C). Line a baking sheet with parchment paper.
> In a large bowl, whisk together the flour, sugar, baking powder, and salt.
> Add the cold, cubed butter to the dry ingredients. Use a pastry cutter or your fingers to cut the butter into the flour mixture until it resembles coarse crumbs.
> Pour in the milk and vanilla extract. Stir until just combined; do not overmix.
> Turn the dough out onto a floured surface and gently knead it a few times until it comes together. Pat the dough into a 3/4-inch thick rectangle.
> Use a round biscuit cutter to cut out shortcakes from the dough. Place them on the prepared baking sheet.
> Bake in the preheated oven for 12-15 minutes or until golden brown. Allow the shortcakes to cool on a wire rack.

For the Strawberries:

> In a bowl, combine sliced strawberries with granulated sugar. Add balsamic vinegar if using. Toss gently and let it sit for about 15-20 minutes to allow the strawberries to release their juices.

For the Whipped Cream:

> In a chilled bowl, whip the heavy cream, powdered sugar, and vanilla extract until stiff peaks form.

Assembling the Strawberry Shortcake:

> Slice each shortcake horizontally. Place a generous spoonful of macerated strawberries on the bottom half.
> Add a dollop of whipped cream and place the other half of the shortcake on top.
> Optionally, garnish with additional strawberries or a dusting of powdered sugar.

Serve and enjoy your delicious Strawberry Shortcake!

Marble Cake

Ingredients:

For the Vanilla Batter:

- 2 ½ cups all-purpose flour
- 2 ½ teaspoons baking powder
- ½ teaspoon salt
- 1 cup unsalted butter, softened
- 2 cups granulated sugar
- 4 large eggs
- 1 teaspoon vanilla extract
- 1 cup whole milk

For the Chocolate Batter:

- 1/3 cup unsweetened cocoa powder
- 1/3 cup hot water
- 1 tablespoon granulated sugar

Instructions:

Preheat your oven to 350°F (175°C). Grease and flour a 10-cup Bundt pan or two 9-inch round cake pans.
In a medium bowl, whisk together the flour, baking powder, and salt. Set aside.
In a large mixing bowl, cream together the softened butter and granulated sugar until light and fluffy.
Add the eggs one at a time, beating well after each addition. Mix in the vanilla extract.
Gradually add the dry ingredients to the wet ingredients, alternating with the milk. Begin and end with the dry ingredients, mixing just until combined.
In a separate bowl, mix the cocoa powder, hot water, and tablespoon of sugar to create a smooth chocolate paste.
Take about 1 ½ to 2 cups of the vanilla batter and mix it with the chocolate paste, creating the chocolate batter.
Spoon alternating dollops of vanilla and chocolate batter into the prepared pan(s).
Use a butter knife to swirl through the batters to create a marbled pattern. Be careful not to overmix; you want a marbled effect.

Bake in the preheated oven for 40-45 minutes (adjust if using two round pans), or until a toothpick inserted into the center comes out clean.

Allow the cake to cool in the pan(s) for 10 minutes, then transfer it to a wire rack to cool completely.

Slice and enjoy your delicious Marble Cake with a perfect blend of vanilla and chocolate flavors!

Pumpkin Spice Cake

Ingredients:

For the Cake:

- 2 ½ cups all-purpose flour
- 2 teaspoons baking powder
- 1 teaspoon baking soda
- ½ teaspoon salt
- 2 teaspoons ground cinnamon
- 1 teaspoon ground ginger
- ½ teaspoon ground nutmeg
- ½ teaspoon ground cloves
- ½ cup unsalted butter, softened
- 1 cup granulated sugar
- 1 cup brown sugar, packed
- 4 large eggs
- 1 can (15 ounces) pumpkin puree
- ½ cup vegetable oil
- 1 teaspoon vanilla extract

For Cream Cheese Frosting:

- 8 ounces (225g) cream cheese, softened
- ½ cup (1 stick) unsalted butter, softened
- 4 cups confectioners' sugar, sifted
- 1 teaspoon vanilla extract

Instructions:

For the Cake:

Preheat your oven to 350°F (175°C). Grease and flour two 9-inch round cake pans.
In a medium bowl, whisk together the flour, baking powder, baking soda, salt, cinnamon, ginger, nutmeg, and cloves. Set aside.
In a large mixing bowl, cream together the softened butter, granulated sugar, and brown sugar until light and fluffy.
Add the eggs one at a time, beating well after each addition. Mix in the pumpkin puree, vegetable oil, and vanilla extract.
Gradually add the dry ingredients to the wet ingredients, mixing just until combined.

Divide the batter evenly between the prepared cake pans and smooth the tops with a spatula.

Bake in the preheated oven for 25-30 minutes or until a toothpick inserted into the center comes out clean.

Allow the cakes to cool in the pans for 10 minutes before transferring them to a wire rack to cool completely.

For Cream Cheese Frosting:

In a large mixing bowl, beat the softened cream cheese and butter until creamy and smooth.

Add the sifted confectioners' sugar and vanilla extract. Beat on low speed until combined, then increase the speed to medium-high and beat until light and fluffy.

Assembling the Cake:

Place one cake layer on a serving plate. Spread a layer of cream cheese frosting on top.

Add the second cake layer and repeat the process.

Use the remaining cream cheese frosting to frost the top and sides of the cake.

Optional: Garnish with a sprinkle of cinnamon or chopped nuts for decoration.

Slice and enjoy your delicious Pumpkin Spice Cake with warm autumn flavors!

Hummingbird Cake

Ingredients:

For the Cake:

- 3 cups all-purpose flour
- 2 cups granulated sugar
- 1 teaspoon baking soda
- 1 teaspoon ground cinnamon
- 1/2 teaspoon salt
- 3 large eggs, beaten
- 1 1/2 cups vegetable oil
- 1 1/2 teaspoons vanilla extract
- 1 can (8 ounces) crushed pineapple, undrained
- 2 cups ripe bananas, mashed (about 4 medium bananas)
- 1 cup chopped pecans or walnuts

For Cream Cheese Frosting:

- 16 ounces (450g) cream cheese, softened
- 1 cup (2 sticks) unsalted butter, softened
- 4 cups confectioners' sugar, sifted
- 1 teaspoon vanilla extract

Instructions:

For the Cake:

Preheat your oven to 350°F (175°C). Grease and flour three 9-inch round cake pans.
In a large bowl, whisk together the flour, sugar, baking soda, cinnamon, and salt.
Add the beaten eggs, vegetable oil, and vanilla extract to the dry ingredients. Mix until well combined.
Stir in the crushed pineapple (with its juice), mashed bananas, and chopped nuts.
Divide the batter evenly among the prepared cake pans and smooth the tops with a spatula.
Bake in the preheated oven for 25-30 minutes or until a toothpick inserted into the center comes out clean.
Allow the cakes to cool in the pans for 10 minutes before transferring them to a wire rack to cool completely.

For Cream Cheese Frosting:

    In a large mixing bowl, beat the softened cream cheese and butter until creamy and smooth.
    Add the sifted confectioners' sugar and vanilla extract. Beat on low speed until combined, then increase the speed to medium-high and beat until light and fluffy.

Assembling the Cake:

    Place one cake layer on a serving plate. Spread a layer of cream cheese frosting on top.
    Add the second cake layer and repeat the process. Place the third layer on top.
    Use the remaining cream cheese frosting to frost the top and sides of the cake.
    Optional: Garnish with chopped nuts or decorate with sliced bananas.

Slice and enjoy your delicious Hummingbird Cake with tropical flavors!

Raspberry Almond Cake

Ingredients:

For the Cake:

- 1 cup unsalted butter, softened
- 1 1/2 cups granulated sugar
- 3 large eggs
- 1 teaspoon almond extract
- 1/2 teaspoon vanilla extract
- 2 cups all-purpose flour
- 1 1/2 teaspoons baking powder
- 1/2 teaspoon baking soda
- 1/4 teaspoon salt
- 1 cup sour cream
- 1 cup fresh raspberries

For the Almond Streusel:

- 1/2 cup sliced almonds
- 1/4 cup granulated sugar
- 2 tablespoons all-purpose flour
- 2 tablespoons unsalted butter, melted
- 1/2 teaspoon almond extract

Instructions:

For the Cake:

Preheat your oven to 350°F (175°C). Grease and flour a 9-inch round cake pan.
In a large mixing bowl, cream together the softened butter and granulated sugar until light and fluffy.
Add the eggs one at a time, beating well after each addition. Mix in the almond extract and vanilla extract.
In a separate bowl, whisk together the flour, baking powder, baking soda, and salt.
Gradually add the dry ingredients to the wet ingredients, alternating with the sour cream. Begin and end with the dry ingredients, mixing just until combined.
Gently fold in the fresh raspberries.
Pour the batter into the prepared cake pan and spread it evenly.

For the Almond Streusel:

> In a small bowl, mix together the sliced almonds, granulated sugar, flour, melted butter, and almond extract until crumbly.
> Sprinkle the almond streusel evenly over the cake batter.
> Bake in the preheated oven for 45-50 minutes or until a toothpick inserted into the center comes out clean.
> Allow the cake to cool in the pan for 15 minutes before transferring it to a wire rack to cool completely.

Slice and enjoy your delicious Raspberry Almond Cake with a delightful almond streusel topping!

Oreo Cheesecake Cake

Ingredients:

For the Chocolate Cake:

- 2 cups all-purpose flour
- 2 cups granulated sugar
- 3/4 cup unsweetened cocoa powder
- 2 teaspoons baking powder
- 1 1/2 teaspoons baking soda
- 1 teaspoon salt
- 2 large eggs
- 1 cup whole milk
- 1/2 cup vegetable oil
- 2 teaspoons vanilla extract
- 1 cup boiling water

For the Oreo Cheesecake Layer:

- 24 ounces (680g) cream cheese, softened
- 1 cup granulated sugar
- 3 large eggs
- 1 teaspoon vanilla extract
- 1 cup crushed Oreo cookies (about 12-15 cookies)

For the Oreo Whipped Cream Frosting:

- 2 cups heavy cream
- 1/2 cup powdered sugar
- 1 teaspoon vanilla extract
- 1 cup crushed Oreo cookies (about 12-15 cookies)

Instructions:

For the Chocolate Cake:

> Preheat your oven to 350°F (175°C). Grease and flour three 9-inch round cake pans. In a large mixing bowl, whisk together the flour, sugar, cocoa powder, baking powder, baking soda, and salt.

Add the eggs, milk, vegetable oil, and vanilla extract to the dry ingredients. Beat on medium speed for 2 minutes.

Stir in the boiling water until the batter is well combined. The batter will be thin.

Divide the batter evenly among the prepared cake pans and smooth the tops with a spatula.

Bake in the preheated oven for 30-35 minutes or until a toothpick inserted into the center comes out clean.

Allow the cakes to cool in the pans for 10 minutes before transferring them to a wire rack to cool completely.

For the Oreo Cheesecake Layer:

Preheat your oven to 325°F (163°C). Grease and line the bottom of a 9-inch springform pan with parchment paper.

In a large mixing bowl, beat the softened cream cheese until smooth.

Add the sugar, eggs, and vanilla extract. Beat until well combined and creamy.

Gently fold in the crushed Oreo cookies.

Pour the Oreo cheesecake batter into the prepared springform pan.

Bake in the preheated oven for 45-50 minutes or until the center is set.

Allow the cheesecake to cool in the pan for 1-2 hours, then refrigerate for at least 4 hours or overnight.

For the Oreo Whipped Cream Frosting:

In a chilled bowl, whip the heavy cream, powdered sugar, and vanilla extract until stiff peaks form.

Gently fold in the crushed Oreo cookies.

Assembling the Cake:

Place one chocolate cake layer on a serving plate. Spread a layer of Oreo whipped cream frosting on top.

Add the Oreo cheesecake layer and repeat the process. Place the third chocolate cake layer on top.

Use the remaining Oreo whipped cream frosting to frost the top and sides of the cake.

Optional: Garnish with additional crushed Oreo cookies on top.

Slice and enjoy your indulgent Oreo Cheesecake Cake!

Mint Chocolate Chip Cake

Ingredients:

For the Chocolate Cake:

- 2 cups all-purpose flour
- 1 3/4 cups granulated sugar
- 3/4 cup unsweetened cocoa powder
- 2 teaspoons baking powder
- 1 1/2 teaspoons baking soda
- 1 teaspoon salt
- 2 large eggs
- 1 cup whole milk
- 1/2 cup vegetable oil
- 2 teaspoons vanilla extract
- 1 cup boiling water

For the Mint Frosting:

- 1 cup unsalted butter, softened
- 4 cups confectioners' sugar, sifted
- 1/4 cup whole milk
- 1 teaspoon mint extract
- Green food coloring (optional)
- 1 cup mini chocolate chips (for decorating)

Instructions:

For the Chocolate Cake:

Preheat your oven to 350°F (175°C). Grease and flour three 8-inch round cake pans.
In a large mixing bowl, whisk together the flour, sugar, cocoa powder, baking powder, baking soda, and salt.
Add the eggs, milk, vegetable oil, and vanilla extract to the dry ingredients. Beat on medium speed for 2 minutes.
Stir in the boiling water until the batter is well combined. The batter will be thin.
Divide the batter evenly among the prepared cake pans and smooth the tops with a spatula.
Bake in the preheated oven for 30-35 minutes or until a toothpick inserted into the center comes out clean.

Allow the cakes to cool in the pans for 10 minutes before transferring them to a wire rack to cool completely.

For the Mint Frosting:

In a large mixing bowl, beat the softened butter until creamy.
Gradually add the sifted confectioners' sugar, alternating with the milk, and beat until smooth and fluffy.
Mix in the mint extract. Add green food coloring if desired, until you achieve the desired shade.

Assembling the Cake:

Place one chocolate cake layer on a serving plate. Spread a layer of mint frosting on top.
Add the second cake layer and repeat the process. Place the third cake layer on top.
Use the remaining mint frosting to frost the top and sides of the cake.
Optional: Press mini chocolate chips onto the sides of the cake for decoration.

Slice and enjoy your refreshing Mint Chocolate Chip Cake!

Peanut Butter Cup Cake

Ingredients:

For the Chocolate Cake:

- 2 cups all-purpose flour
- 1 3/4 cups granulated sugar
- 3/4 cup unsweetened cocoa powder
- 2 teaspoons baking powder
- 1 1/2 teaspoons baking soda
- 1 teaspoon salt
- 2 large eggs
- 1 cup whole milk
- 1/2 cup vegetable oil
- 2 teaspoons vanilla extract
- 1 cup boiling water

For the Peanut Butter Frosting:

- 1 cup unsalted butter, softened
- 1 cup creamy peanut butter
- 4 cups confectioners' sugar, sifted
- 1/4 cup whole milk
- 1 teaspoon vanilla extract

For the Chocolate Ganache:

- 1 cup semisweet chocolate chips
- 1/2 cup heavy cream

For Garnish:

- Mini peanut butter cups, chopped

Instructions:

For the Chocolate Cake:

Preheat your oven to 350°F (175°C). Grease and flour three 8-inch round cake pans.

In a large mixing bowl, whisk together the flour, sugar, cocoa powder, baking powder, baking soda, and salt.

Add the eggs, milk, vegetable oil, and vanilla extract to the dry ingredients. Beat on medium speed for 2 minutes.

Stir in the boiling water until the batter is well combined. The batter will be thin.

Divide the batter evenly among the prepared cake pans and smooth the tops with a spatula.

Bake in the preheated oven for 30-35 minutes or until a toothpick inserted into the center comes out clean.

Allow the cakes to cool in the pans for 10 minutes before transferring them to a wire rack to cool completely.

For the Peanut Butter Frosting:

In a large mixing bowl, beat the softened butter and peanut butter until creamy.

Gradually add the sifted confectioners' sugar, alternating with the milk, and beat until smooth and fluffy.

Mix in the vanilla extract.

For the Chocolate Ganache:

In a small saucepan, heat the heavy cream until it just begins to simmer.

Pour the hot cream over the chocolate chips. Let it sit for a minute, then stir until smooth and glossy.

Assembling the Cake:

Place one chocolate cake layer on a serving plate. Spread a layer of peanut butter frosting on top.

Add the second cake layer and repeat the process. Place the third cake layer on top.

Use the remaining peanut butter frosting to frost the top and sides of the cake.

Pour the chocolate ganache over the top of the cake, letting it drip down the sides.

Garnish with chopped mini peanut butter cups.

Slice and enjoy your indulgent Peanut Butter Cup Cake!

Tiramisu Cake

Ingredients:

For the Sponge Cake:

- 2 cups all-purpose flour
- 2 teaspoons baking powder
- 1/2 teaspoon baking soda
- 1/4 teaspoon salt
- 1/2 cup unsalted butter, softened
- 1 cup granulated sugar
- 3 large eggs
- 1 teaspoon vanilla extract
- 1 cup buttermilk, at room temperature

For the Coffee Soaking Syrup:

- 1 cup strong brewed coffee, cooled
- 2 tablespoons coffee liqueur (optional)
- 2 tablespoons sugar

For the Mascarpone Filling:

- 8 ounces (225g) mascarpone cheese, softened
- 1 cup heavy cream
- 1 cup confectioners' sugar, sifted
- 1 teaspoon vanilla extract

For Dusting:

- Cocoa powder

Instructions:

For the Sponge Cake:

> Preheat your oven to 350°F (175°C). Grease and flour two 9-inch round cake pans. In a medium bowl, whisk together the flour, baking powder, baking soda, and salt. Set aside.

In a large mixing bowl, cream together the softened butter and granulated sugar until light and fluffy.

Add the eggs one at a time, beating well after each addition. Mix in the vanilla extract.

Gradually add the dry ingredients to the wet ingredients, alternating with the buttermilk. Begin and end with the dry ingredients, mixing just until combined.

Divide the batter evenly between the prepared cake pans and smooth the tops with a spatula.

Bake in the preheated oven for 25-30 minutes or until a toothpick inserted into the center comes out clean.

Allow the cakes to cool in the pans for 10 minutes before transferring them to a wire rack to cool completely.

For the Coffee Soaking Syrup:

In a bowl, mix together the brewed coffee, coffee liqueur (if using), and sugar until the sugar is dissolved. Set aside.

For the Mascarpone Filling:

In a mixing bowl, beat the mascarpone cheese until smooth.

In a separate bowl, whip the heavy cream until soft peaks form. Add the confectioners' sugar and vanilla extract, and continue whipping until stiff peaks form.

Gently fold the whipped cream into the mascarpone cheese until well combined.

Assembling the Tiramisu Cake:

Place one sponge cake layer on a serving plate. Brush with a generous amount of the coffee soaking syrup.

Spread a layer of the mascarpone filling over the soaked cake layer.

Place the second cake layer on top and repeat the process.

Use a spatula to smooth the filling on the top and sides of the cake.

Dust the top of the cake with cocoa powder.

Refrigerate the Tiramisu Cake for at least 4 hours or overnight before serving.

Slice and enjoy your delectable Tiramisu Cake!

Caramel Apple Cake

Ingredients:

For the Cake:

- 2 cups all-purpose flour
- 1 1/2 teaspoons baking soda
- 1 teaspoon ground cinnamon
- 1/2 teaspoon ground nutmeg
- 1/2 teaspoon salt
- 1/2 cup unsalted butter, softened
- 1 cup granulated sugar
- 1/2 cup brown sugar, packed
- 2 large eggs
- 1 teaspoon vanilla extract
- 1 cup sour cream
- 2 cups peeled and finely chopped apples (about 2 medium apples)

For the Caramel Sauce:

- 1 cup granulated sugar
- 1/4 cup water
- 1/2 cup heavy cream
- 2 tablespoons unsalted butter
- 1/2 teaspoon vanilla extract
- 1/4 teaspoon salt

For Cream Cheese Frosting:

- 8 ounces (225g) cream cheese, softened
- 1/2 cup (1 stick) unsalted butter, softened
- 4 cups confectioners' sugar, sifted
- 1 teaspoon vanilla extract

Instructions:

For the Cake:

Preheat your oven to 350°F (175°C). Grease and flour a 9x13-inch baking pan.

In a medium bowl, whisk together the flour, baking soda, cinnamon, nutmeg, and salt. Set aside.

In a large mixing bowl, cream together the softened butter, granulated sugar, and brown sugar until light and fluffy.

Add the eggs one at a time, beating well after each addition. Mix in the vanilla extract.

Gradually add the dry ingredients to the wet ingredients, alternating with the sour cream. Begin and end with the dry ingredients, mixing just until combined.

Fold in the finely chopped apples.

Spread the batter evenly in the prepared baking pan.

Bake in the preheated oven for 35-40 minutes or until a toothpick inserted into the center comes out clean.

Allow the cake to cool in the pan for 10 minutes before transferring it to a wire rack to cool completely.

For the Caramel Sauce:

In a medium saucepan, combine the granulated sugar and water. Cook over medium heat, swirling the pan occasionally, until the sugar dissolves and turns amber in color.

Carefully whisk in the heavy cream, butter, vanilla extract, and salt. Continue to cook, whisking constantly, until the mixture is smooth. Remove from heat and let it cool.

For Cream Cheese Frosting:

In a large mixing bowl, beat the softened cream cheese and butter until creamy and smooth.

Add the sifted confectioners' sugar and vanilla extract. Beat on low speed until combined, then increase the speed to medium-high and beat until light and fluffy.

Assembling the Cake:

Drizzle the cooled caramel sauce over the cooled apple cake.

Spread a layer of cream cheese frosting over the caramel drizzle.

Optional: Drizzle additional caramel sauce over the cream cheese frosting for decoration.

Slice and enjoy your scrumptious Caramel Apple Cake!

Cherry Chocolate Cake

Ingredients:

For the Chocolate Cake:

- 2 cups all-purpose flour
- 1 3/4 cups granulated sugar
- 3/4 cup unsweetened cocoa powder
- 2 teaspoons baking powder
- 1 1/2 teaspoons baking soda
- 1 teaspoon salt
- 2 large eggs
- 1 cup whole milk
- 1/2 cup vegetable oil
- 2 teaspoons vanilla extract
- 1 cup boiling water

For the Cherry Filling:

- 2 cups fresh or frozen cherries, pitted and halved
- 1/2 cup granulated sugar
- 2 tablespoons cornstarch
- 1 tablespoon lemon juice

For the Chocolate Ganache:

- 1 cup semisweet chocolate chips
- 1/2 cup heavy cream

For Garnish:

- Fresh cherries, for decoration

Instructions:

For the Chocolate Cake:

Preheat your oven to 350°F (175°C). Grease and flour two 9-inch round cake pans. In a large mixing bowl, whisk together the flour, sugar, cocoa powder, baking powder, baking soda, and salt.

Add the eggs, milk, vegetable oil, and vanilla extract to the dry ingredients. Beat on medium speed for 2 minutes.
Stir in the boiling water until the batter is well combined. The batter will be thin.
Divide the batter evenly among the prepared cake pans and smooth the tops with a spatula.
Bake in the preheated oven for 30-35 minutes or until a toothpick inserted into the center comes out clean.
Allow the cakes to cool in the pans for 10 minutes before transferring them to a wire rack to cool completely.

For the Cherry Filling:

In a saucepan, combine the cherries, sugar, cornstarch, and lemon juice. Cook over medium heat, stirring constantly, until the mixture thickens and the cherries release their juices. Remove from heat and let it cool.

For the Chocolate Ganache:

In a small saucepan, heat the heavy cream until it just begins to simmer.
Pour the hot cream over the chocolate chips. Let it sit for a minute, then stir until smooth and glossy.

Assembling the Cake:

Place one chocolate cake layer on a serving plate. Spread a layer of chocolate ganache over the cake.
Spoon the cherry filling over the ganache.
Place the second cake layer on top and repeat the process.
Use the remaining chocolate ganache to frost the top and sides of the cake.
Garnish with fresh cherries on top for decoration.

Slice and enjoy your delightful Cherry Chocolate Cake!

Almond Joy Cake Recipe:

Ingredients:

For the Chocolate Cake:

- 2 cups all-purpose flour
- 1 3/4 cups granulated sugar

- 3/4 cup unsweetened cocoa powder
- 2 teaspoons baking powder
- 1 1/2 teaspoons baking soda
- 1 teaspoon salt
- 2 large eggs
- 1 cup whole milk
- 1/2 cup vegetable oil
- 2 teaspoons vanilla extract
- 1 cup boiling water

For the Coconut Filling:

- 2 cups sweetened shredded coconut
- 1 can (14 ounces) sweetened condensed milk
- 1/2 cup unsalted butter, melted
- 1 teaspoon vanilla extract

For the Chocolate Ganache:

- 1 cup semisweet chocolate chips
- 1/2 cup heavy cream

For Garnish:

- Sliced almonds
- Additional shredded coconut

Instructions:

For the Chocolate Cake:

> Preheat your oven to 350°F (175°C). Grease and flour two 9-inch round cake pans.
> In a large mixing bowl, whisk together the flour, sugar, cocoa powder, baking powder, baking soda, and salt.
> Add the eggs, milk, vegetable oil, and vanilla extract to the dry ingredients. Beat on medium speed for 2 minutes.
> Stir in the boiling water until the batter is well combined. The batter will be thin.
> Divide the batter evenly among the prepared cake pans and smooth the tops with a spatula.
> Bake in the preheated oven for 30-35 minutes or until a toothpick inserted into the center comes out clean.

Allow the cakes to cool in the pans for 10 minutes before transferring them to a wire rack to cool completely.

For the Coconut Filling:

In a bowl, combine the shredded coconut, sweetened condensed milk, melted butter, and vanilla extract. Mix until well combined.

For the Chocolate Ganache:

In a small saucepan, heat the heavy cream until it just begins to simmer.
Pour the hot cream over the chocolate chips. Let it sit for a minute, then stir until smooth and glossy.

Assembling the Cake:

Place one chocolate cake layer on a serving plate. Spread a layer of the coconut filling over the cake.
Place the second cake layer on top and repeat the process.
Pour the chocolate ganache over the top of the cake, letting it drip down the sides.
Garnish with sliced almonds and additional shredded coconut.

Slice and enjoy your decadent Almond Joy Cake!

Lavender Lemon Cake

Ingredients:

For the Cake:

- 2 1/2 cups all-purpose flour
- 2 teaspoons baking powder
- 1/2 teaspoon baking soda
- 1/2 teaspoon salt
- 1 tablespoon dried culinary lavender buds (food-grade)
- 1 cup unsalted butter, softened
- 2 cups granulated sugar
- 4 large eggs
- 1 teaspoon vanilla extract
- 1 cup buttermilk
- Zest of 2 lemons

For the Lavender Lemon Syrup:

- 1/4 cup fresh lemon juice
- 1/4 cup granulated sugar
- 1 tablespoon dried culinary lavender buds (food-grade)

For the Lavender Lemon Frosting:

- 1 cup unsalted butter, softened
- 4 cups confectioners' sugar, sifted
- 2 tablespoons fresh lemon juice
- 1 tablespoon dried culinary lavender buds (food-grade)
- Zest of 1 lemon
- Purple food coloring (optional)

Instructions:

For the Cake:

Preheat your oven to 350°F (175°C). Grease and flour three 8-inch round cake pans. In a medium bowl, whisk together the flour, baking powder, baking soda, and salt. Add the dried lavender buds and whisk to combine. Set aside.

In a large mixing bowl, cream together the softened butter and granulated sugar until light and fluffy.

Add the eggs one at a time, beating well after each addition. Mix in the vanilla extract.

Gradually add the dry ingredients to the wet ingredients, alternating with the buttermilk. Begin and end with the dry ingredients, mixing just until combined.

Stir in the lemon zest.

Divide the batter evenly among the prepared cake pans and smooth the tops with a spatula.

Bake in the preheated oven for 25-30 minutes or until a toothpick inserted into the center comes out clean.

Allow the cakes to cool in the pans for 10 minutes before transferring them to a wire rack to cool completely.

For the Lavender Lemon Syrup:

In a small saucepan, combine the lemon juice, sugar, and dried lavender buds. Heat over medium heat until the sugar dissolves and the mixture simmers for a few minutes.

Remove from heat and let it cool.

Strain out the lavender buds, leaving a fragrant lemon syrup.

For the Lavender Lemon Frosting:

In a large mixing bowl, beat the softened butter until creamy.

Gradually add the sifted confectioners' sugar, alternating with the fresh lemon juice. Beat until smooth and fluffy.

Stir in the dried lavender buds, lemon zest, and purple food coloring if desired.

Assembling the Cake:

Place one cake layer on a serving plate. Brush a generous amount of the lavender lemon syrup over the top.

Spread a layer of lavender lemon frosting over the syrup-soaked cake layer.

Place the second cake layer on top and repeat the process.

Add the third cake layer and frost the top and sides of the entire cake with the lavender lemon frosting.

Optional: Garnish with additional dried lavender buds or lemon zest for decoration.

Slice and enjoy your delightful Lavender Lemon Cake with a touch of floral and citrus flavors!

Maple Pecan Cake

Ingredients:

For the Cake:

- 2 cups all-purpose flour
- 1 1/2 teaspoons baking powder
- 1/2 teaspoon baking soda
- 1/2 teaspoon salt
- 1 cup unsalted butter, softened
- 1 cup granulated sugar
- 1 cup brown sugar, packed
- 4 large eggs
- 1 teaspoon vanilla extract
- 1 cup buttermilk

For the Maple Pecan Filling:

- 1 cup chopped pecans
- 1/4 cup unsalted butter
- 1/2 cup brown sugar, packed
- 1/4 cup maple syrup
- 1/4 cup heavy cream

For the Maple Cream Cheese Frosting:

- 8 ounces (225g) cream cheese, softened
- 1/2 cup (1 stick) unsalted butter, softened
- 1/4 cup maple syrup
- 4 cups confectioners' sugar, sifted
- 1 teaspoon vanilla extract

For Garnish:

- Chopped pecans

Instructions:

For the Cake:

Preheat your oven to 350°F (175°C). Grease and flour three 8-inch round cake pans.

In a medium bowl, whisk together the flour, baking powder, baking soda, and salt. Set aside.

In a large mixing bowl, cream together the softened butter, granulated sugar, and brown sugar until light and fluffy.

Add the eggs one at a time, beating well after each addition. Mix in the vanilla extract.

Gradually add the dry ingredients to the wet ingredients, alternating with the buttermilk. Begin and end with the dry ingredients, mixing just until combined.

Divide the batter evenly among the prepared cake pans and smooth the tops with a spatula.

Bake in the preheated oven for 25-30 minutes or until a toothpick inserted into the center comes out clean.

Allow the cakes to cool in the pans for 10 minutes before transferring them to a wire rack to cool completely.

For the Maple Pecan Filling:

In a saucepan over medium heat, melt the butter. Add the chopped pecans and brown sugar. Cook, stirring frequently, until the sugar is dissolved.

Stir in the maple syrup and heavy cream. Continue to cook until the mixture thickens slightly. Remove from heat and let it cool.

For the Maple Cream Cheese Frosting:

In a large mixing bowl, beat the softened cream cheese and butter until creamy.

Gradually add the sifted confectioners' sugar, alternating with the maple syrup. Beat until smooth and fluffy.

Mix in the vanilla extract.

Assembling the Cake:

Place one cake layer on a serving plate. Spread a layer of the maple pecan filling over the cake.

Add the second cake layer and repeat the process. Place the third cake layer on top.

Use the maple cream cheese frosting to frost the top and sides of the cake.

Garnish with chopped pecans on top.

Slice and enjoy your delicious Maple Pecan Cake with rich flavors of maple and pecans!

Coffee and Walnut Cake

Ingredients:

For the Cake:

- 1 cup unsalted butter, softened
- 1 cup granulated sugar
- 4 large eggs
- 2 cups all-purpose flour
- 2 teaspoons baking powder
- 1/2 cup chopped walnuts
- 2 tablespoons instant coffee dissolved in 2 tablespoons hot water (cooled)

For the Coffee Buttercream:

- 1 cup unsalted butter, softened
- 2 cups confectioners' sugar, sifted
- 2 tablespoons instant coffee dissolved in 1 tablespoon hot water (cooled)

For Garnish:

- Chopped walnuts

Instructions:

For the Cake:

Preheat your oven to 350°F (175°C). Grease and line two 8-inch round cake pans with parchment paper.
In a large mixing bowl, cream together the softened butter and granulated sugar until light and fluffy.
Add the eggs one at a time, beating well after each addition.
In a separate bowl, whisk together the flour and baking powder.
Gradually add the dry ingredients to the wet ingredients, mixing until just combined.
Fold in the chopped walnuts.
Add the dissolved instant coffee to the batter and mix until well incorporated.

Divide the batter evenly between the prepared cake pans and smooth the tops.

Bake in the preheated oven for 25-30 minutes or until a toothpick inserted into the center comes out clean.

Allow the cakes to cool in the pans for 10 minutes before transferring them to a wire rack to cool completely.

For the Coffee Buttercream:

In a large mixing bowl, beat the softened butter until creamy.

Gradually add the sifted confectioners' sugar, alternating with the dissolved instant coffee. Beat until smooth and fluffy.

Assembling the Cake:

Place one cake layer on a serving plate. Spread a layer of coffee buttercream over the top.

Add the second cake layer and repeat the process.

Use the remaining coffee buttercream to frost the top and sides of the cake.

Garnish with chopped walnuts on top.

Slice and enjoy your classic Coffee and Walnut Cake with a rich coffee flavor and the crunch of walnuts!

Mango Coconut Cake

Ingredients:

For the Cake:

- 2 cups all-purpose flour
- 1 1/2 teaspoons baking powder
- 1/2 teaspoon baking soda
- 1/4 teaspoon salt
- 1/2 cup unsalted butter, softened
- 1 cup granulated sugar
- 2 large eggs
- 1 teaspoon vanilla extract
- 1 cup buttermilk
- 1 cup ripe mango puree (from about 2 medium-sized mangoes)

For the Mango Coconut Frosting:

- 1 cup unsalted butter, softened
- 4 cups confectioners' sugar, sifted
- 1/2 cup ripe mango puree
- 1 teaspoon coconut extract
- Shredded coconut, for garnish

For Garnish:

- Sliced mangoes
- Toasted coconut flakes

Instructions:

For the Cake:

> Preheat your oven to 350°F (175°C). Grease and flour two 9-inch round cake pans.
> In a medium bowl, whisk together the flour, baking powder, baking soda, and salt. Set aside.
> In a large mixing bowl, cream together the softened butter and granulated sugar until light and fluffy.
> Add the eggs one at a time, beating well after each addition. Mix in the vanilla extract.

Gradually add the dry ingredients to the wet ingredients, alternating with the buttermilk. Begin and end with the dry ingredients, mixing just until combined.

Stir in the ripe mango puree until well incorporated.

Divide the batter evenly between the prepared cake pans and smooth the tops with a spatula.

Bake in the preheated oven for 25-30 minutes or until a toothpick inserted into the center comes out clean.

Allow the cakes to cool in the pans for 10 minutes before transferring them to a wire rack to cool completely.

For the Mango Coconut Frosting:

In a large mixing bowl, beat the softened butter until creamy.

Gradually add the sifted confectioners' sugar, alternating with the ripe mango puree and coconut extract. Beat until smooth and fluffy.

Assembling the Cake:

Place one cake layer on a serving plate. Spread a layer of mango coconut frosting over the top.

Add the second cake layer and repeat the process.

Use the remaining mango coconut frosting to frost the top and sides of the cake.

Garnish with sliced mangoes and toasted coconut flakes.

Slice and enjoy your tropical-inspired Mango Coconut Cake with the delightful flavors of mango and coconut!

Hazelnut Chocolate Cake

Ingredients:

For the Chocolate Hazelnut Cake:

- 1 cup unsalted butter, softened
- 1 cup granulated sugar
- 4 large eggs
- 1 teaspoon vanilla extract
- 1 cup all-purpose flour
- 1/2 cup cocoa powder
- 1 teaspoon baking powder
- 1/2 teaspoon baking soda
- 1/2 teaspoon salt
- 1 cup finely ground hazelnuts
- 1 cup buttermilk

For the Chocolate Hazelnut Frosting:

- 1/2 cup unsalted butter, softened
- 1 cup chocolate hazelnut spread (such as Nutella)
- 2 cups confectioners' sugar, sifted
- 1 teaspoon vanilla extract
- 2-3 tablespoons heavy cream

For Garnish:

- Chopped hazelnuts
- Chocolate shavings

Instructions:

For the Chocolate Hazelnut Cake:

Preheat your oven to 350°F (175°C). Grease and flour two 9-inch round cake pans.

In a large mixing bowl, cream together the softened butter and granulated sugar until light and fluffy.

Add the eggs one at a time, beating well after each addition. Mix in the vanilla extract.

In a separate bowl, whisk together the flour, cocoa powder, baking powder, baking soda, and salt.

Gradually add the dry ingredients to the wet ingredients, alternating with the buttermilk. Begin and end with the dry ingredients, mixing just until combined.

Fold in the finely ground hazelnuts.

Divide the batter evenly between the prepared cake pans and smooth the tops with a spatula.

Bake in the preheated oven for 25-30 minutes or until a toothpick inserted into the center comes out clean.

Allow the cakes to cool in the pans for 10 minutes before transferring them to a wire rack to cool completely.

For the Chocolate Hazelnut Frosting:

In a large mixing bowl, beat the softened butter until creamy.

Add the chocolate hazelnut spread and beat until well combined.

Gradually add the sifted confectioners' sugar, mixing until smooth.

Mix in the vanilla extract.

Add heavy cream, one tablespoon at a time, until the frosting reaches a spreadable consistency.

Assembling the Cake:

Place one chocolate hazelnut cake layer on a serving plate. Spread a layer of chocolate hazelnut frosting over the top.

Add the second cake layer and repeat the process.

Use the remaining chocolate hazelnut frosting to frost the top and sides of the cake.

Garnish with chopped hazelnuts and chocolate shavings.

Slice and enjoy your decadent Hazelnut Chocolate Cake with the rich flavors of hazelnuts and chocolate!

Cinnamon Roll Cake

Ingredients:

For the Cake:

- 2 cups all-purpose flour
- 1 cup granulated sugar
- 1 tablespoon baking powder
- 1/2 teaspoon salt
- 1 cup milk
- 2 large eggs
- 1 teaspoon vanilla extract
- 1/2 cup unsalted butter, melted

For the Cinnamon Swirl:

- 1/2 cup unsalted butter, softened
- 1 cup brown sugar, packed
- 2 tablespoons all-purpose flour
- 1 tablespoon ground cinnamon

For the Cream Cheese Frosting:

- 4 ounces (113g) cream cheese, softened
- 1/4 cup unsalted butter, softened
- 1 cup confectioners' sugar, sifted
- 1/2 teaspoon vanilla extract

Instructions:

For the Cake:

Preheat your oven to 350°F (175°C). Grease a 9x13-inch baking pan.

In a large mixing bowl, whisk together the flour, sugar, baking powder, and salt.

In a separate bowl, whisk together the milk, eggs, and vanilla extract.

Pour the wet ingredients into the dry ingredients and stir until just combined.

Stir in the melted butter until the batter is smooth.

Pour the batter into the prepared baking pan, spreading it evenly.

For the Cinnamon Swirl:

In a bowl, mix together the softened butter, brown sugar, flour, and ground cinnamon until well combined.

Drop spoonfuls of the cinnamon swirl mixture onto the cake batter.

Use a knife to swirl the cinnamon mixture into the batter, creating a marbled effect.

Bake in the preheated oven for 25-30 minutes or until a toothpick inserted into the center comes out clean.

For the Cream Cheese Frosting:

In a mixing bowl, beat together the softened cream cheese and butter until smooth.

Gradually add the sifted confectioners' sugar and vanilla extract. Beat until creamy and well combined.

Assembling the Cake:

Allow the cake to cool for a few minutes before spreading the cream cheese frosting over the warm cake.

Optionally, drizzle additional cinnamon swirl mixture on top for extra flavor.

Slice and serve warm. Enjoy your delightful Cinnamon Roll Cake!

This cake captures the essence of cinnamon rolls with a moist cake, a cinnamon swirl, and a creamy cream cheese frosting.

Guinness Chocolate Cake

Ingredients:

For the Cake:

- 1 cup Guinness stout
- 1 cup unsalted butter
- 3/4 cup unsweetened cocoa powder
- 2 cups all-purpose flour
- 2 cups granulated sugar
- 1 1/2 teaspoons baking soda
- 3/4 teaspoon salt
- 2 large eggs
- 2/3 cup sour cream

For the Cream Cheese Frosting:

- 8 ounces (225g) cream cheese, softened
- 1 1/2 cups confectioners' sugar, sifted
- 1/2 cup unsalted butter, softened
- 2 teaspoons vanilla extract

Instructions:

For the Cake:

Preheat your oven to 350°F (175°C). Grease and flour a 9x13-inch baking pan.

In a saucepan, heat the Guinness and unsalted butter over medium heat until the butter is melted.

Whisk in the cocoa powder until smooth. Remove from heat and let it cool.

In a large mixing bowl, whisk together the flour, sugar, baking soda, and salt.

In a separate bowl, beat the eggs and sour cream together.

Pour the Guinness mixture into the flour mixture and stir until just combined.

Add the egg and sour cream mixture and mix until smooth.

Pour the batter into the prepared baking pan.

Bake in the preheated oven for 30-35 minutes or until a toothpick inserted into the center comes out clean.

Allow the cake to cool completely before frosting.

For the Cream Cheese Frosting:

In a mixing bowl, beat together the softened cream cheese, confectioners' sugar, softened butter, and vanilla extract until smooth and creamy.

Spread the cream cheese frosting over the cooled cake.

Optionally, you can decorate the cake with chocolate shavings or cocoa powder.

Slice and enjoy your rich and moist Guinness Chocolate Cake with luscious cream cheese frosting! The addition of Guinness adds depth and flavor to the chocolate cake.

Chai Spiced Cake

Ingredients:

For the Cake:

- 2 1/2 cups all-purpose flour
- 2 teaspoons baking powder
- 1/2 teaspoon baking soda
- 1/2 teaspoon salt
- 2 teaspoons ground cinnamon
- 1 teaspoon ground ginger
- 1 teaspoon ground cardamom
- 1/2 teaspoon ground cloves
- 1/2 teaspoon ground nutmeg
- 1 cup unsalted butter, softened
- 1 1/2 cups granulated sugar
- 4 large eggs
- 1 teaspoon vanilla extract
- 1 1/4 cups buttermilk

For the Chai Spiced Cream Cheese Frosting:

- 8 ounces (225g) cream cheese, softened
- 1/2 cup unsalted butter, softened
- 4 cups confectioners' sugar, sifted
- 1 teaspoon ground cinnamon
- 1/2 teaspoon ground ginger
- 1/2 teaspoon ground cardamom

- 1/4 teaspoon ground cloves
- 1/4 teaspoon ground nutmeg
- 1 teaspoon vanilla extract

Instructions:

For the Cake:

Preheat your oven to 350°F (175°C). Grease and flour two 9-inch round cake pans.

In a medium bowl, whisk together the flour, baking powder, baking soda, salt, and the chai spices (cinnamon, ginger, cardamom, cloves, nutmeg). Set aside.

In a large mixing bowl, cream together the softened butter and granulated sugar until light and fluffy.

Add the eggs one at a time, beating well after each addition. Mix in the vanilla extract.

Gradually add the dry ingredients to the wet ingredients, alternating with the buttermilk. Begin and end with the dry ingredients, mixing just until combined.

Divide the batter evenly between the prepared cake pans and smooth the tops with a spatula.

Bake in the preheated oven for 25-30 minutes or until a toothpick inserted into the center comes out clean.

Allow the cakes to cool in the pans for 10 minutes before transferring them to a wire rack to cool completely.

For the Chai Spiced Cream Cheese Frosting:

In a large mixing bowl, beat together the softened cream cheese and butter until creamy. Gradually add the sifted confectioners' sugar, chai spices, and vanilla extract. Beat until smooth and fluffy.

Assembling the Cake:

>Place one chai spiced cake layer on a serving plate. Spread a layer of chai spiced cream cheese frosting over the top.
>
>Add the second cake layer and repeat the process.
>
>Use the remaining chai spiced cream cheese frosting to frost the top and sides of the cake.
>
>Optionally, you can garnish the cake with a sprinkle of chai spices or chopped nuts.

Slice and enjoy your delicious Chai Spiced Cake with warm and aromatic flavors!

Cranberry Orange Cake

Ingredients:

For the Cake:

- 2 cups all-purpose flour
- 1 1/2 teaspoons baking powder
- 1/2 teaspoon baking soda
- 1/4 teaspoon salt
- 1 cup unsalted butter, softened
- 1 cup granulated sugar
- 3 large eggs
- 1 teaspoon vanilla extract
- 1 cup sour cream
- Zest of 1 orange
- 2 cups fresh or frozen cranberries

For the Orange Glaze:

- 1 cup confectioners' sugar, sifted
- 2 tablespoons fresh orange juice
- Zest of 1 orange

Instructions:

For the Cake:

Preheat your oven to 350°F (175°C). Grease and flour a 9x13-inch baking pan.

In a medium bowl, whisk together the flour, baking powder, baking soda, and salt. Set aside.

In a large mixing bowl, cream together the softened butter and granulated sugar until light and fluffy.

Add the eggs one at a time, beating well after each addition. Mix in the vanilla extract.

Gradually add the dry ingredients to the wet ingredients, alternating with the sour cream. Begin and end with the dry ingredients, mixing just until combined.

Stir in the orange zest.

Gently fold in the cranberries.

Spread the batter evenly in the prepared baking pan.

Bake in the preheated oven for 35-40 minutes or until a toothpick inserted into the center comes out clean.

Allow the cake to cool completely in the pan on a wire rack.

For the Orange Glaze:

In a small bowl, whisk together the sifted confectioners' sugar, fresh orange juice, and orange zest until smooth.

Drizzle the orange glaze over the cooled cake.

Optionally, garnish with additional orange zest for a burst of flavor.

Slice and enjoy your moist and flavorful Cranberry Orange Cake with a hint of citrus sweetness!

Rum Raisin Cake

Ingredients:

For the Rum-Soaked Raisins:

- 1 cup raisins
- 1/2 cup dark rum

For the Cake:

- 2 cups all-purpose flour
- 1 1/2 teaspoons baking powder
- 1/2 teaspoon baking soda
- 1/4 teaspoon salt
- 1 cup unsalted butter, softened
- 1 cup granulated sugar
- 3 large eggs
- 1 teaspoon vanilla extract
- 1 cup sour cream
- Rum-soaked raisins (from above)

For the Rum Glaze:

- 1/4 cup unsalted butter
- 1/4 cup granulated sugar
- 1/4 cup dark rum

Instructions:

For the Rum-Soaked Raisins:

In a small saucepan, heat the dark rum until warm but not boiling.

Place the raisins in a bowl and pour the warm rum over them. Let them soak for at least 1-2 hours or overnight. Drain the excess rum before using.

For the Cake:

Preheat your oven to 350°F (175°C). Grease and flour a 9x13-inch baking pan.

In a medium bowl, whisk together the flour, baking powder, baking soda, and salt. Set aside.

In a large mixing bowl, cream together the softened butter and granulated sugar until light and fluffy.

Add the eggs one at a time, beating well after each addition. Mix in the vanilla extract.

Gradually add the dry ingredients to the wet ingredients, alternating with the sour cream. Begin and end with the dry ingredients, mixing just until combined.

Gently fold in the rum-soaked raisins.

Spread the batter evenly in the prepared baking pan.

Bake in the preheated oven for 30-35 minutes or until a toothpick inserted into the center comes out clean.

Allow the cake to cool in the pan on a wire rack.

For the Rum Glaze:

In a saucepan, melt the unsalted butter over medium heat.

Stir in the granulated sugar and dark rum. Bring to a gentle simmer and let it cook for a few minutes until the sugar is dissolved and the glaze thickens slightly.

Assembling the Cake:

While the cake is still warm, poke holes in the top using a skewer or fork.

Pour the warm rum glaze over the cake, allowing it to soak in.

Let the cake cool completely before slicing and serving.

Enjoy your moist and flavorful Rum Raisin Cake with the rich essence of rum-soaked raisins and a delicious rum glaze!

Black Forest Cake

Ingredients:

For the Chocolate Cake:

- 2 cups all-purpose flour
- 2 cups granulated sugar
- 3/4 cup unsweetened cocoa powder
- 2 teaspoons baking powder
- 1 1/2 teaspoons baking soda
- 1 teaspoon salt
- 2 large eggs
- 1 cup whole milk
- 1/2 cup vegetable oil
- 2 teaspoons vanilla extract
- 1 cup boiling water

For the Cherry Filling:

- 1 can (21 ounces) cherry pie filling

For the Whipped Cream Frosting:

- 2 cups heavy cream, chilled
- 1/2 cup confectioners' sugar
- 1 teaspoon vanilla extract

For Garnish:

- Dark chocolate shavings
- Maraschino cherries

Instructions:

For the Chocolate Cake:

Preheat your oven to 350°F (175°C). Grease and flour two 9-inch round cake pans.

In a large mixing bowl, whisk together the flour, sugar, cocoa powder, baking powder, baking soda, and salt.

Add the eggs, milk, vegetable oil, and vanilla extract to the dry ingredients. Beat on medium speed for 2 minutes.

Stir in the boiling water until the batter is well combined. The batter will be thin.

Divide the batter evenly among the prepared cake pans and smooth the tops with a spatula.

Bake in the preheated oven for 30-35 minutes or until a toothpick inserted into the center comes out clean.

Allow the cakes to cool in the pans for 10 minutes before transferring them to a wire rack to cool completely.

For the Whipped Cream Frosting:

In a chilled mixing bowl, beat the heavy cream, confectioners' sugar, and vanilla extract until stiff peaks form.

Assembling the Black Forest Cake:

Place one chocolate cake layer on a serving plate. Spread a layer of whipped cream frosting over the cake.

Spoon half of the cherry pie filling over the whipped cream layer.

Place the second cake layer on top and repeat the process, finishing with a layer of whipped cream frosting and cherry pie filling on top.

Use the remaining whipped cream to frost the sides of the cake.

Garnish with dark chocolate shavings and maraschino cherries on top.

Slice and enjoy your classic Black Forest Cake with layers of chocolate cake, whipped cream, and cherry filling!

Passion Fruit Cake

Ingredients:

For the Cake:

- 2 cups all-purpose flour
- 2 teaspoons baking powder
- 1/2 teaspoon baking soda
- 1/4 teaspoon salt
- 1 cup unsalted butter, softened
- 1 1/2 cups granulated sugar
- 4 large eggs
- 1 teaspoon vanilla extract
- 1 cup passion fruit puree (strained to remove seeds)

For the Passion Fruit Glaze:

- 1/2 cup passion fruit puree (strained)
- 1 cup confectioners' sugar, sifted

Instructions:

For the Cake:

>Preheat your oven to 350°F (175°C). Grease and flour two 9-inch round cake pans.
>
>In a medium bowl, whisk together the flour, baking powder, baking soda, and salt. Set aside.
>
>In a large mixing bowl, cream together the softened butter and granulated sugar until light and fluffy.

Add the eggs one at a time, beating well after each addition. Mix in the vanilla extract. Gradually add the dry ingredients to the wet ingredients, alternating with the passion fruit puree. Begin and end with the dry ingredients, mixing just until combined.

Divide the batter evenly between the prepared cake pans and smooth the tops with a spatula.

Bake in the preheated oven for 25-30 minutes or until a toothpick inserted into the center comes out clean.

Allow the cakes to cool in the pans for 10 minutes before transferring them to a wire rack to cool completely.

For the Passion Fruit Glaze:

In a small bowl, whisk together the strained passion fruit puree and confectioners' sugar until smooth.

Assembling the Cake:

Place one passion fruit cake layer on a serving plate. Drizzle a portion of the passion fruit glaze over the top.

Add the second cake layer and repeat the process.

Use the remaining passion fruit glaze to cover the top of the cake.

Optionally, garnish with additional passion fruit seeds or slices for decoration.

Slice and enjoy your tropical-inspired Passion Fruit Cake with the exotic flavor of passion fruit!

Pistachio Rose Cake

Ingredients:

For the Pistachio Cake:

- 1 cup unsalted pistachios, shelled
- 2 cups all-purpose flour
- 2 teaspoons baking powder
- 1/2 teaspoon baking soda
- 1/2 teaspoon salt
- 1 cup unsalted butter, softened
- 1 1/2 cups granulated sugar
- 4 large eggs
- 1 teaspoon vanilla extract
- 1 cup buttermilk

For the Rosewater Buttercream:

- 1 cup unsalted butter, softened
- 4 cups confectioners' sugar, sifted
- 2-3 tablespoons rosewater (adjust to taste)
- Pink food coloring (optional)
- Crushed pistachios for garnish

Instructions:

For the Pistachio Cake:

Preheat your oven to 350°F (175°C). Grease and flour two 9-inch round cake pans.

In a food processor, pulse the shelled pistachios until finely ground. Be careful not to over-process, as you don't want to turn them into paste.

In a medium bowl, whisk together the ground pistachios, flour, baking powder, baking soda, and salt. Set aside.

In a large mixing bowl, cream together the softened butter and granulated sugar until light and fluffy.

Add the eggs one at a time, beating well after each addition. Mix in the vanilla extract.

Gradually add the dry ingredients to the wet ingredients, alternating with the buttermilk. Begin and end with the dry ingredients, mixing just until combined.

Divide the batter evenly between the prepared cake pans and smooth the tops with a spatula.

Bake in the preheated oven for 25-30 minutes or until a toothpick inserted into the center comes out clean.

Allow the cakes to cool in the pans for 10 minutes before transferring them to a wire rack to cool completely.

For the Rosewater Buttercream:

In a large mixing bowl, beat the softened butter until creamy.

Gradually add the sifted confectioners' sugar, alternating with the rosewater. Adjust the amount of rosewater to your taste.

If desired, add a few drops of pink food coloring to achieve a light pink color. Beat until smooth and fluffy.

Assembling the Cake:

Place one pistachio cake layer on a serving plate. Spread a layer of rosewater buttercream over the cake.

Add the second cake layer and repeat the process.

Use the remaining rosewater buttercream to frost the top and sides of the cake.

Garnish with crushed pistachios on top.

Slice and enjoy your Pistachio Rose Cake with the delightful combination of pistachio and rose flavors!

S'mores Cake

Ingredients:

For the Chocolate Cake:

- 2 cups all-purpose flour
- 1 3/4 cups granulated sugar
- 3/4 cup unsweetened cocoa powder
- 2 teaspoons baking powder
- 1 1/2 teaspoons baking soda
- 1 teaspoon salt
- 2 large eggs
- 1 cup whole milk
- 1/2 cup vegetable oil
- 2 teaspoons vanilla extract
- 1 cup boiling water

For the Graham Cracker Crust:

- 1 1/2 cups graham cracker crumbs
- 1/4 cup granulated sugar
- 1/2 cup unsalted butter, melted

For the Marshmallow Frosting:

- 4 large egg whites
- 1 cup granulated sugar
- 1/4 teaspoon cream of tartar

- 1 teaspoon vanilla extract

For Garnish:

- Chocolate shavings
- Mini marshmallows
- Crushed graham crackers

Instructions:

For the Chocolate Cake:

Preheat your oven to 350°F (175°C). Grease and flour two 9-inch round cake pans.

In a large mixing bowl, whisk together the flour, sugar, cocoa powder, baking powder, baking soda, and salt.

Add the eggs, milk, vegetable oil, and vanilla extract to the dry ingredients. Beat on medium speed for 2 minutes.

Stir in the boiling water until the batter is well combined. The batter will be thin.

Divide the batter evenly among the prepared cake pans and smooth the tops with a spatula.

Bake in the preheated oven for 30-35 minutes or until a toothpick inserted into the center comes out clean.

Allow the cakes to cool in the pans for 10 minutes before transferring them to a wire rack to cool completely.

For the Graham Cracker Crust:

In a bowl, mix together the graham cracker crumbs, sugar, and melted butter until well combined.

Press the mixture into the bottom of a 9-inch springform pan to create the crust.

For the Marshmallow Frosting:

In a heatproof bowl, whisk together the egg whites, sugar, and cream of tartar.

Place the bowl over a pot of simmering water (double boiler) and whisk constantly until the sugar is dissolved and the mixture reaches 160°F (71°C).

Remove from heat and transfer the mixture to a stand mixer.

Beat on high speed until stiff peaks form and the bowl is cool to the touch.

Mix in the vanilla extract.

Assembling the S'mores Cake:

Place one chocolate cake layer on top of the graham cracker crust in the springform pan.

Spread a layer of marshmallow frosting over the cake layer.

Add the second chocolate cake layer and cover the top with marshmallow frosting.

Optionally, use a kitchen torch to lightly toast the marshmallow frosting.

Garnish with chocolate shavings, mini marshmallows, and crushed graham crackers.

Chill the cake in the refrigerator for a few hours before serving. Slice and enjoy your indulgent S'mores Cake!

Buttermilk Honey Cake

Ingredients:

For the Cake:

- 2 1/2 cups all-purpose flour
- 1 1/2 teaspoons baking powder
- 1/2 teaspoon baking soda
- 1/2 teaspoon salt
- 1 cup unsalted butter, softened
- 1 cup granulated sugar
- 1/2 cup honey
- 3 large eggs
- 1 teaspoon vanilla extract
- 1 1/2 cups buttermilk

For the Honey Glaze:

- 1/4 cup unsalted butter
- 1/4 cup honey
- 1/2 cup confectioners' sugar, sifted
- 1/2 teaspoon vanilla extract

Instructions:

For the Cake:

Preheat your oven to 350°F (175°C). Grease and flour a 9x13-inch baking pan.

In a medium bowl, whisk together the flour, baking powder, baking soda, and salt. Set aside.

In a large mixing bowl, cream together the softened butter, granulated sugar, and honey until light and fluffy.

Add the eggs one at a time, beating well after each addition. Mix in the vanilla extract.

Gradually add the dry ingredients to the wet ingredients, alternating with the buttermilk. Begin and end with the dry ingredients, mixing just until combined.

Pour the batter into the prepared baking pan, spreading it evenly.

Bake in the preheated oven for 25-30 minutes or until a toothpick inserted into the center comes out clean.

Allow the cake to cool in the pan on a wire rack.

For the Honey Glaze:

In a small saucepan, melt the butter over medium heat.

Stir in the honey, confectioners' sugar, and vanilla extract until well combined.

Pour the honey glaze over the cooled cake, spreading it evenly.

Allow the glaze to set before slicing and serving.

Slice and enjoy your Buttermilk Honey Cake with a sweet and moist crumb, complemented by the rich flavor of honey!

Matcha Green Tea Cake

Ingredients:

For the Matcha Cake:

- 2 cups all-purpose flour
- 2 tablespoons matcha green tea powder
- 1 1/2 teaspoons baking powder
- 1/2 teaspoon baking soda
- 1/4 teaspoon salt
- 1 cup unsalted butter, softened
- 1 1/2 cups granulated sugar
- 3 large eggs
- 1 teaspoon vanilla extract
- 1 cup buttermilk

For the Matcha Cream Cheese Frosting:

- 8 ounces (225g) cream cheese, softened
- 1/2 cup unsalted butter, softened
- 2 cups confectioners' sugar, sifted
- 1 tablespoon matcha green tea powder
- 1 teaspoon vanilla extract

For Garnish (Optional):

- Matcha powder for dusting
- Edible flowers or berries

Instructions:

For the Matcha Cake:

Preheat your oven to 350°F (175°C). Grease and flour two 9-inch round cake pans.

In a medium bowl, whisk together the flour, matcha powder, baking powder, baking soda, and salt. Set aside.

In a large mixing bowl, cream together the softened butter and granulated sugar until light and fluffy.

Add the eggs one at a time, beating well after each addition. Mix in the vanilla extract.

Gradually add the dry ingredients to the wet ingredients, alternating with the buttermilk. Begin and end with the dry ingredients, mixing just until combined.

Divide the batter evenly between the prepared cake pans and smooth the tops with a spatula.

Bake in the preheated oven for 25-30 minutes or until a toothpick inserted into the center comes out clean.

Allow the cakes to cool in the pans for 10 minutes before transferring them to a wire rack to cool completely.

For the Matcha Cream Cheese Frosting:

In a large mixing bowl, beat together the softened cream cheese and butter until smooth. Gradually add the sifted confectioners' sugar, matcha powder, and vanilla extract. Beat until smooth and fluffy.

Assembling the Matcha Green Tea Cake:

Place one matcha cake layer on a serving plate. Spread a layer of matcha cream cheese frosting over the cake.

Add the second cake layer and repeat the process.

Use the remaining matcha cream cheese frosting to frost the top and sides of the cake.

Optionally, dust the top with matcha powder and garnish with edible flowers or berries.

Slice and enjoy your Matcha Green Tea Cake with its vibrant color and rich matcha flavor!

Pineapple Upside-Down Cake

Ingredients:

For the Topping:

- 1/2 cup unsalted butter
- 1 cup brown sugar, packed
- 1 can (20 ounces) pineapple slices, drained
- Maraschino cherries, for decoration

For the Cake Batter:

- 1 1/2 cups all-purpose flour
- 1 1/2 teaspoons baking powder
- 1/4 teaspoon salt
- 1/2 cup unsalted butter, softened
- 1 cup granulated sugar
- 2 large eggs
- 1 teaspoon vanilla extract
- 3/4 cup milk

Instructions:

Preheat your oven to 350°F (175°C). Grease a 9-inch round cake pan.

In a small saucepan, melt the 1/2 cup of butter over medium heat. Stir in the brown sugar until well combined.

Pour the melted butter and brown sugar mixture into the bottom of the greased cake pan.

Arrange the pineapple slices on top of the butter and sugar mixture. Place a maraschino cherry in the center of each pineapple slice.

In a medium bowl, whisk together the flour, baking powder, and salt. Set aside.

In a large mixing bowl, cream together the softened butter and granulated sugar until light and fluffy.

Add the eggs one at a time, beating well after each addition. Mix in the vanilla extract.

Gradually add the dry ingredients to the wet ingredients, alternating with the milk. Begin and end with the dry ingredients, mixing just until combined.

Pour the batter over the arranged pineapple slices in the cake pan, spreading it evenly.

Bake in the preheated oven for 30-35 minutes or until a toothpick inserted into the center comes out clean.

Allow the cake to cool in the pan for about 10 minutes.

Invert the cake onto a serving plate, allowing the pineapple slices to be on top.

Let the cake cool completely before slicing and serving.

Enjoy your classic Pineapple Upside-Down Cake with its delicious caramelized pineapple and cherry topping!

Lemon Poppy Seed Cake

Ingredients:

For the Cake:

- 2 1/2 cups all-purpose flour
- 2 tablespoons poppy seeds
- 1 1/2 teaspoons baking powder
- 1/2 teaspoon baking soda
- 1/4 teaspoon salt
- 1 cup unsalted butter, softened
- 2 cups granulated sugar
- 4 large eggs
- 1 teaspoon vanilla extract
- 1 tablespoon lemon zest
- 1/4 cup fresh lemon juice
- 1 cup buttermilk

For the Lemon Glaze:

- 1 cup confectioners' sugar, sifted
- 2 tablespoons fresh lemon juice
- 1 teaspoon lemon zest

Instructions:

For the Cake:

Preheat your oven to 350°F (175°C). Grease and flour a 9x13-inch baking pan.

In a medium bowl, whisk together the flour, poppy seeds, baking powder, baking soda, and salt. Set aside.

In a large mixing bowl, cream together the softened butter and granulated sugar until light and fluffy.

Add the eggs one at a time, beating well after each addition. Mix in the vanilla extract.

Stir in the lemon zest and lemon juice.

Gradually add the dry ingredients to the wet ingredients, alternating with the buttermilk. Begin and end with the dry ingredients, mixing just until combined.

Pour the batter into the prepared baking pan, spreading it evenly.

Bake in the preheated oven for 30-35 minutes or until a toothpick inserted into the center comes out clean.

Allow the cake to cool in the pan for about 10 minutes before transferring it to a wire rack to cool completely.

For the Lemon Glaze:

In a small bowl, whisk together the sifted confectioners' sugar, fresh lemon juice, and lemon zest until smooth.

Drizzle the lemon glaze over the cooled cake.

Optionally, you can garnish with additional lemon zest for a burst of citrus flavor.

Slice and enjoy your moist and flavorful Lemon Poppy Seed Cake with a tangy lemon glaze!

Cappuccino Cake

Ingredients:

For the Cake:

- 2 cups all-purpose flour
- 1 1/2 teaspoons baking powder
- 1/2 teaspoon baking soda
- 1/2 teaspoon salt
- 1/2 cup unsalted butter, softened
- 1 1/2 cups granulated sugar
- 3 large eggs
- 2 teaspoons instant coffee granules dissolved in 1 tablespoon hot water
- 1 cup buttermilk
- 1 teaspoon vanilla extract

For the Cappuccino Buttercream:

- 1 cup unsalted butter, softened
- 4 cups confectioners' sugar, sifted
- 2 tablespoons cocoa powder
- 2 tablespoons instant coffee granules dissolved in 2 tablespoons hot water
- 1 teaspoon vanilla extract
- Pinch of salt

For Garnish (Optional):

- Chocolate-covered coffee beans

- Cocoa powder for dusting

Instructions:

For the Cake:

Preheat your oven to 350°F (175°C). Grease and flour two 9-inch round cake pans.

In a medium bowl, whisk together the flour, baking powder, baking soda, and salt. Set aside.

In a large mixing bowl, cream together the softened butter and granulated sugar until light and fluffy.

Add the eggs one at a time, beating well after each addition.

Mix the instant coffee granules with hot water to dissolve them. Add the coffee mixture to the batter and mix well.

Gradually add the dry ingredients to the wet ingredients, alternating with buttermilk.

Begin and end with the dry ingredients, mixing just until combined.

Stir in the vanilla extract.

Divide the batter evenly between the prepared cake pans and smooth the tops with a spatula.

Bake in the preheated oven for 25-30 minutes or until a toothpick inserted into the center comes out clean.

Allow the cakes to cool in the pans for 10 minutes before transferring them to a wire rack to cool completely.

For the Cappuccino Buttercream:

In a large mixing bowl, beat the softened butter until creamy.

Gradually add the sifted confectioners' sugar, cocoa powder, dissolved instant coffee, vanilla extract, and a pinch of salt. Beat until smooth and fluffy.

Assembling the Cappuccino Cake:

Place one cappuccino cake layer on a serving plate. Spread a layer of cappuccino buttercream over the cake.

Add the second cake layer and repeat the process.

Use the remaining cappuccino buttercream to frost the top and sides of the cake.

Optionally, garnish with chocolate-covered coffee beans and dust with cocoa powder.

Slice and enjoy your rich and indulgent Cappuccino Cake with the perfect blend of coffee flavors!

Chocolate Raspberry Cake

Ingredients:

For the Chocolate Cake:

- 1 3/4 cups all-purpose flour
- 1 1/2 teaspoons baking powder
- 1 1/2 teaspoons baking soda
- 3/4 cup unsweetened cocoa powder
- 2 cups granulated sugar
- 1/2 teaspoon salt
- 2 large eggs
- 1 cup whole milk
- 1/2 cup vegetable oil
- 2 teaspoons vanilla extract
- 1 cup boiling water

For the Raspberry Filling:

- 2 cups fresh raspberries
- 1/4 cup granulated sugar
- 1 tablespoon cornstarch
- 1 tablespoon lemon juice

For the Chocolate Ganache:

- 1 cup semi-sweet chocolate chips
- 1/2 cup heavy cream

For Garnish:

- Fresh raspberries
- Chocolate shavings

Instructions:

For the Chocolate Cake:

Preheat your oven to 350°F (175°C). Grease and flour two 9-inch round cake pans.

In a large mixing bowl, whisk together the flour, baking powder, baking soda, cocoa powder, sugar, and salt.

Add the eggs, milk, vegetable oil, and vanilla extract to the dry ingredients. Beat on medium speed for 2 minutes.

Stir in the boiling water until the batter is well combined. The batter will be thin.

Divide the batter evenly among the prepared cake pans and smooth the tops with a spatula.

Bake in the preheated oven for 30-35 minutes or until a toothpick inserted into the center comes out clean.

Allow the cakes to cool in the pans for 10 minutes before transferring them to a wire rack to cool completely.

For the Raspberry Filling:

In a saucepan, combine the fresh raspberries, sugar, cornstarch, and lemon juice.

Cook over medium heat, stirring frequently, until the mixture thickens and the raspberries break down. Remove from heat and let it cool.

For the Chocolate Ganache:

In a heatproof bowl, combine the chocolate chips and heavy cream.

Microwave in 20-second intervals, stirring each time until the chocolate is melted and the mixture is smooth.

Assembling the Chocolate Raspberry Cake:

Place one chocolate cake layer on a serving plate. Spread a layer of raspberry filling over the cake.

Add the second cake layer and repeat the process.

Pour the chocolate ganache over the top of the cake, allowing it to drip down the sides.

Garnish with fresh raspberries and chocolate shavings.

Slice and enjoy your decadent Chocolate Raspberry Cake with the perfect combination of rich chocolate and tangy raspberry flavors!

Key Lime Pie Cake

Ingredients:

For the Cake:

- 2 1/2 cups all-purpose flour
- 2 1/2 teaspoons baking powder
- 1/2 teaspoon baking soda
- 1/2 teaspoon salt
- 1 cup unsalted butter, softened
- 1 3/4 cups granulated sugar
- 4 large eggs
- 1 teaspoon vanilla extract
- 1 tablespoon key lime zest (from about 10 key limes)
- 1/2 cup key lime juice (freshly squeezed)

For the Key Lime Cream Cheese Frosting:

- 8 ounces cream cheese, softened
- 1/2 cup unsalted butter, softened
- 4 cups confectioners' sugar, sifted
- 1 tablespoon key lime juice
- 1 tablespoon key lime zest

For Garnish:

- Additional key lime zest
- Lime slices or wedges

Instructions:

For the Cake:

Preheat your oven to 350°F (175°C). Grease and flour two 9-inch round cake pans.

In a medium bowl, whisk together the flour, baking powder, baking soda, and salt. Set aside.

In a large mixing bowl, cream together the softened butter and granulated sugar until light and fluffy.

Add the eggs one at a time, beating well after each addition. Mix in the vanilla extract.

Stir in the key lime zest and key lime juice.

Gradually add the dry ingredients to the wet ingredients, mixing just until combined.

Divide the batter evenly between the prepared cake pans and smooth the tops with a spatula.

Bake in the preheated oven for 25-30 minutes or until a toothpick inserted into the center comes out clean.

Allow the cakes to cool in the pans for 10 minutes before transferring them to a wire rack to cool completely.

For the Key Lime Cream Cheese Frosting:

In a large mixing bowl, beat together the softened cream cheese and butter until smooth.

Gradually add the sifted confectioners' sugar, key lime juice, and key lime zest. Beat until smooth and fluffy.

Assembling the Key Lime Pie Cake:

Place one key lime cake layer on a serving plate. Spread a layer of key lime cream cheese frosting over the cake.

Add the second cake layer and repeat the process.

Use the remaining key lime cream cheese frosting to frost the top and sides of the cake.

Garnish with additional key lime zest and lime slices or wedges.

Slice and enjoy your refreshing Key Lime Pie Cake with its citrusy and creamy goodness!

Mocha Hazelnut Cake

Ingredients:

For the Cake:

- 1 3/4 cups all-purpose flour
- 1 1/2 teaspoons baking powder
- 1/2 teaspoon baking soda
- 1/4 teaspoon salt
- 1/2 cup unsalted butter, softened
- 1 cup granulated sugar
- 2 large eggs
- 1 teaspoon vanilla extract
- 1/2 cup buttermilk
- 1/2 cup strong brewed coffee, cooled
- 1/4 cup unsweetened cocoa powder
- 1/2 cup finely chopped hazelnuts, toasted

For the Mocha Hazelnut Frosting:

- 1 cup unsalted butter, softened
- 2 cups confectioners' sugar, sifted
- 2 tablespoons unsweetened cocoa powder
- 1 tablespoon instant coffee granules dissolved in 1 tablespoon hot water
- 1 teaspoon vanilla extract
- 1/4 cup finely chopped hazelnuts, toasted

Instructions:

For the Cake:

Preheat your oven to 350°F (175°C). Grease and flour two 9-inch round cake pans.

In a medium bowl, whisk together the flour, baking powder, baking soda, and salt. Set aside.

In a large mixing bowl, cream together the softened butter and granulated sugar until light and fluffy.

Add the eggs one at a time, beating well after each addition. Mix in the vanilla extract.

In a separate bowl, combine the buttermilk and brewed coffee.

Gradually add the dry ingredients to the wet ingredients, alternating with the buttermilk-coffee mixture. Begin and end with the dry ingredients, mixing just until combined.

Divide the batter evenly between the prepared cake pans and smooth the tops with a spatula.

Bake in the preheated oven for 25-30 minutes or until a toothpick inserted into the center comes out clean.

Allow the cakes to cool in the pans for 10 minutes before transferring them to a wire rack to cool completely.

For the Mocha Hazelnut Frosting:

In a large mixing bowl, beat the softened butter until creamy.

Gradually add the sifted confectioners' sugar, cocoa powder, dissolved instant coffee, and vanilla extract. Beat until smooth and fluffy.

Assembling the Mocha Hazelnut Cake:

Place one mocha hazelnut cake layer on a serving plate. Spread a layer of mocha hazelnut frosting over the cake.

Add the second cake layer and repeat the process.

Use the remaining mocha hazelnut frosting to frost the top and sides of the cake.

Sprinkle finely chopped hazelnuts on top for garnish.

Slice and enjoy your heavenly Mocha Hazelnut Cake with the perfect blend of coffee, chocolate, and hazelnut flavors!

Banana Nutella Cake

Ingredients:

For the Cake:

- 2 cups all-purpose flour
- 1 1/2 teaspoons baking powder
- 1/2 teaspoon baking soda
- 1/4 teaspoon salt
- 1/2 cup unsalted butter, softened
- 1 cup granulated sugar
- 2 large eggs
- 1 teaspoon vanilla extract
- 3 ripe bananas, mashed
- 1/2 cup sour cream

For the Nutella Swirl:

- 1/2 cup Nutella

For the Nutella Frosting:

- 1 cup unsalted butter, softened
- 1 cup Nutella
- 2 cups confectioners' sugar, sifted
- 2 tablespoons milk
- 1 teaspoon vanilla extract

For Garnish:

- Sliced bananas
- Chopped hazelnuts

Instructions:

For the Cake:

Preheat your oven to 350°F (175°C). Grease and flour a 9x13-inch baking pan.

In a medium bowl, whisk together the flour, baking powder, baking soda, and salt. Set aside.

In a large mixing bowl, cream together the softened butter and granulated sugar until light and fluffy.

Add the eggs one at a time, beating well after each addition. Mix in the vanilla extract.

Stir in the mashed bananas and sour cream.

Gradually add the dry ingredients to the wet ingredients, mixing just until combined.

Pour half of the batter into the prepared baking pan and spread it evenly.

Drop spoonfuls of Nutella over the batter. Use a knife to swirl the Nutella into the batter.

Add the remaining batter over the Nutella layer and spread it evenly.

Drop more spoonfuls of Nutella on top and swirl it again with a knife.

Bake in the preheated oven for 30-35 minutes or until a toothpick inserted into the center comes out clean.

Allow the cake to cool in the pan for about 10 minutes before transferring it to a wire rack to cool completely.

For the Nutella Frosting:

In a large mixing bowl, beat together the softened butter and Nutella until smooth.

Gradually add the sifted confectioners' sugar, milk, and vanilla extract. Beat until smooth and creamy.

Assembling the Banana Nutella Cake:

Once the cake is completely cooled, spread the Nutella frosting over the top. Garnish with sliced bananas and chopped hazelnuts.

Slice and enjoy your Banana Nutella Cake with the irresistible combination of banana and Nutella flavors!

Mint Oreo Cake

Ingredients:

For the Chocolate Mint Cake:

- 2 cups all-purpose flour
- 1 3/4 cups granulated sugar
- 3/4 cup unsweetened cocoa powder
- 2 teaspoons baking powder
- 1/2 teaspoon baking soda
- 1/2 teaspoon salt
- 1 cup unsalted butter, softened
- 4 large eggs
- 1 teaspoon vanilla extract
- 1 1/2 teaspoons mint extract
- 1 1/4 cups buttermilk

For the Mint Oreo Buttercream:

- 1 cup unsalted butter, softened
- 4 cups confectioners' sugar, sifted
- 2 tablespoons milk
- 1 teaspoon mint extract
- Green food coloring (optional)
- 1 cup crushed Mint Oreo cookies (for frosting and decoration)

For Garnish:

- Mint Oreo cookies
- Fresh mint leaves (optional)

Instructions:

For the Chocolate Mint Cake:

> Preheat your oven to 350°F (175°C). Grease and flour two 9-inch round cake pans.
>
> In a large bowl, whisk together the flour, sugar, cocoa powder, baking powder, baking soda, and salt.
>
> Add the softened butter, eggs, vanilla extract, mint extract, and buttermilk. Mix on medium speed until well combined.
>
> Divide the batter evenly between the prepared cake pans and smooth the tops with a spatula.
>
> Bake in the preheated oven for 25-30 minutes or until a toothpick inserted into the center comes out clean.
>
> Allow the cakes to cool in the pans for 10 minutes before transferring them to a wire rack to cool completely.

For the Mint Oreo Buttercream:

> In a large mixing bowl, beat the softened butter until creamy.
>
> Gradually add the sifted confectioners' sugar, milk, mint extract, and green food coloring (if using). Beat until smooth and fluffy.
>
> Fold in the crushed Mint Oreo cookies, reserving some for decoration.

Assembling the Mint Oreo Cake:

Place one chocolate mint cake layer on a serving plate. Spread a layer of mint Oreo buttercream over the cake.

Add the second cake layer and repeat the process.

Use the remaining mint Oreo buttercream to frost the top and sides of the cake.

Decorate the top of the cake with Mint Oreo cookies and the reserved crushed cookies.

Optionally, garnish with fresh mint leaves for a vibrant touch.

Slice and enjoy your Mint Oreo Cake with its rich chocolate-mint flavor and delightful Oreo crunch!

Caramel Macchiato Cake

Ingredients:

For the Coffee Cake:

- 2 cups all-purpose flour
- 1 1/2 teaspoons baking powder
- 1/2 teaspoon baking soda
- 1/4 teaspoon salt
- 1 cup unsalted butter, softened
- 1 1/2 cups granulated sugar
- 3 large eggs
- 1 teaspoon vanilla extract
- 1 cup strong brewed coffee, cooled

For the Caramel Sauce:

- 1 cup granulated sugar
- 1/4 cup water
- 1/2 cup heavy cream
- 2 tablespoons unsalted butter
- 1 teaspoon vanilla extract
- Pinch of salt

For the Coffee Buttercream:

- 1 cup unsalted butter, softened
- 4 cups confectioners' sugar, sifted

- 2 tablespoons instant coffee granules dissolved in 2 tablespoons hot water
- 1 teaspoon vanilla extract

For Garnish:

- Caramel sauce
- Coffee beans (optional)

Instructions:

For the Coffee Cake:

Preheat your oven to 350°F (175°C). Grease and flour two 9-inch round cake pans.

In a medium bowl, whisk together the flour, baking powder, baking soda, and salt. Set aside.

In a large mixing bowl, cream together the softened butter and granulated sugar until light and fluffy.

Add the eggs one at a time, beating well after each addition. Mix in the vanilla extract.

Gradually add the dry ingredients to the wet ingredients, alternating with the brewed coffee. Begin and end with the dry ingredients, mixing just until combined.

Divide the batter evenly between the prepared cake pans and smooth the tops with a spatula.

Bake in the preheated oven for 25-30 minutes or until a toothpick inserted into the center comes out clean.

Allow the cakes to cool in the pans for 10 minutes before transferring them to a wire rack to cool completely.

For the Caramel Sauce:

In a saucepan, combine the granulated sugar and water. Cook over medium heat, swirling the pan occasionally until the sugar dissolves and turns into a golden caramel color. Remove the pan from heat and carefully add the heavy cream, butter, vanilla extract, and a pinch of salt. Stir until smooth. Allow it to cool.

For the Coffee Buttercream:

In a large mixing bowl, beat the softened butter until creamy.

Gradually add the sifted confectioners' sugar, dissolved instant coffee, and vanilla extract. Beat until smooth and fluffy.

Assembling the Caramel Macchiato Cake:

Place one coffee cake layer on a serving plate. Spread a layer of coffee buttercream over the cake.

Drizzle some caramel sauce over the buttercream.

Add the second cake layer and repeat the process.

Use the remaining coffee buttercream to frost the top and sides of the cake.

Drizzle additional caramel sauce over the top for a marbled effect.

Optionally, garnish with coffee beans.

Slice and enjoy your indulgent Caramel Macchiato Cake with its delicious combination of coffee and caramel flavors!

Gingerbread Cake

Ingredients:

For the Cake:

- 2 1/2 cups all-purpose flour
- 2 teaspoons ground ginger
- 1 1/2 teaspoons ground cinnamon
- 1/2 teaspoon ground nutmeg
- 1/2 teaspoon ground cloves
- 1/2 teaspoon baking powder
- 1/2 teaspoon baking soda
- 1/4 teaspoon salt
- 1/2 cup unsalted butter, softened
- 1/2 cup dark brown sugar, packed
- 1/2 cup molasses
- 2 large eggs
- 1 cup hot water

For the Cream Cheese Frosting:

- 8 ounces cream cheese, softened
- 1/2 cup unsalted butter, softened
- 4 cups confectioners' sugar, sifted
- 1 teaspoon vanilla extract

For Garnish:

- Crystallized ginger or chopped nuts (optional)

Instructions:

For the Gingerbread Cake:

Preheat your oven to 350°F (175°C). Grease and flour a 9x13-inch baking pan.

In a medium bowl, whisk together the flour, ground ginger, ground cinnamon, ground nutmeg, ground cloves, baking powder, baking soda, and salt. Set aside.

In a large mixing bowl, cream together the softened butter and dark brown sugar until light and fluffy.

Add the molasses and mix until well combined.

Add the eggs one at a time, beating well after each addition.

Gradually add the dry ingredients to the wet ingredients, mixing just until combined.

Slowly pour in the hot water and mix until the batter is smooth.

Pour the batter into the prepared baking pan, spreading it evenly.

Bake in the preheated oven for 30-35 minutes or until a toothpick inserted into the center comes out clean.

Allow the cake to cool in the pan for about 10 minutes before transferring it to a wire rack to cool completely.

For the Cream Cheese Frosting:

In a large mixing bowl, beat together the softened cream cheese and butter until smooth.

Gradually add the sifted confectioners' sugar and vanilla extract. Beat until smooth and creamy.

Assembling the Gingerbread Cake:

Once the cake is completely cooled, spread the cream cheese frosting over the top. Optionally, garnish with crystallized ginger or chopped nuts for added texture.

Slice and enjoy your moist and flavorful Gingerbread Cake with the warm and comforting spices of ginger, cinnamon, and cloves!

Chocolate Peanut Butter Cake

Ingredients:

For the Chocolate Cake:

- 2 cups all-purpose flour
- 1 3/4 cups granulated sugar
- 3/4 cup unsweetened cocoa powder
- 2 teaspoons baking powder
- 1 1/2 teaspoons baking soda
- 1/2 teaspoon salt
- 1 cup buttermilk
- 1/2 cup vegetable oil
- 2 large eggs
- 2 teaspoons vanilla extract
- 1 cup boiling water

For the Peanut Butter Frosting:

- 1 cup unsalted butter, softened
- 1 cup creamy peanut butter
- 4 cups confectioners' sugar, sifted
- 1/4 cup milk
- 1 teaspoon vanilla extract

For the Chocolate Ganache:

- 1/2 cup heavy cream

- 1 cup semi-sweet chocolate chips

For Garnish:

- Chopped peanuts
- Peanut butter cups (optional)

Instructions:

For the Chocolate Cake:

Preheat your oven to 350°F (175°C). Grease and flour two 9-inch round cake pans.

In a large bowl, whisk together the flour, sugar, cocoa powder, baking powder, baking soda, and salt.

Add the buttermilk, vegetable oil, eggs, and vanilla extract. Mix on medium speed until well combined.

Gradually add the boiling water, mixing until the batter is smooth. The batter will be thin.

Divide the batter evenly between the prepared cake pans and smooth the tops with a spatula.

Bake in the preheated oven for 30-35 minutes or until a toothpick inserted into the center comes out clean.

Allow the cakes to cool in the pans for 10 minutes before transferring them to a wire rack to cool completely.

For the Peanut Butter Frosting:

In a large mixing bowl, beat together the softened butter and peanut butter until creamy.

Gradually add the sifted confectioners' sugar, milk, and vanilla extract. Beat until smooth and fluffy.

For the Chocolate Ganache:

In a saucepan, heat the heavy cream until it just starts to boil.

Pour the hot cream over the chocolate chips and let it sit for a minute. Stir until smooth.

Assembling the Chocolate Peanut Butter Cake:

Place one chocolate cake layer on a serving plate. Spread a layer of peanut butter frosting over the cake.

Add the second cake layer and repeat the process.

Use the remaining peanut butter frosting to frost the top and sides of the cake.

Pour the chocolate ganache over the top, allowing it to drip down the sides.

Optionally, garnish with chopped peanuts and peanut butter cups.

Slice and enjoy your decadent Chocolate Peanut Butter Cake with the perfect balance of rich chocolate and creamy peanut butter!

www.ingramcontent.com/pod-product-compliance
Lightning Source LLC
LaVergne TN
LVHW061938070526
838199LV00060B/3869

9 798869 138194